Learn from Scratch

Large Language Model

Learn from Scratch

Large Language Model

By Manish Soni

SHROFF PUBLISHERS & DISTRIBUTORS PVT.LTD.
Navi Mumbai

Large Language Model for Beginners

By Content Team of Lightup Technologies

Series Editor: Manish Soni

First Edition: April 2025

ISBN: 978-93-5542-726-7

Printed at Decora Book Prints Pvt. Ltd., Mumbai • Published by Shroff Publishers and Distributors Pvt. Ltd. B-103, Railway Commercial Complex, Sector 3, Sanpada (E), Navi Mumbai 400705 • Tel: (91 22) 4158 4158 WhatsApp +91 7304487700 4158 4141 • E-mail: spdorders@shroffpublishers.com • URL: www.shroffpublishers.com

Preface

More than a decade ago, my journey into AI began with a class on statistical pattern classification, which led to my first independent project: creating a model and web application to detect a song's mood based on its lyrics. Since then, language models have continued to capture my interest.

With the release of ChatGPT in 2022, Large Language Model s (LLMs) have made a transformative impact, reshaping the way many of us work. These models are incredibly versatile, taking on tasks such as grammar checking, email composition, document summarisation, and more. Their ability to understand and generate human-like text has applications across numerous fields, from customer service to content creation to technical domains like coding and data analysis. One defining feature of LLMs is their size—they contain millions or even billions of parameters. By comparison, more traditional Machine Learning methods can classify the Iris flower dataset with high accuracy using a model with only two parameters. Despite their size, however, LLMs don't have to be mysterious or inaccessible.

This book will guide you through building an LLM from the ground up, giving you a solid understanding of the inner workings of models like those used in ChatGPT. Gaining confidence in the fundamental concepts and code behind LLMs is essential, not just for debugging and optimizing, but for experimenting with new ideas as well.

In my own early work with LLMs, I spent years sifting through research papers and piecing together code to understand these models. My goal with this book is to simplify that process by offering a step-by-step tutorial covering each major component and phase of LLM development.

I firmly believe that the best way to understand LLMs is to build one from scratch truly- and you'll find it can be a lot of fun too!

Happy reading and coding!

I am reachable on social Media as below. Please join me for better Networking.

https://www.linkedin.com/in/computersirmanish

https://www.facebook.com/profile.php?id=100086949087962

https://www.instagram.com/manishsoniitbooksauthor

https://x.com/ManishS37126872

https://www.reddit.com/user/ManishTheAuthor/

https://www.quora.com/profile/Manish-Soni-1815

Regards,

Manish Soni

M. Phil., MCA, M. Sc., B. Sc.

PMP, PMI-ACP, PRINCE2, CSM, SAFe POPM, PSM1, ITIL, ITSM, OCA, MCDBA, SCJP, MCPDEA,

MCSE, CCNA, PMI CD, Certified Software Manager, Lean Six Sigma, Microsoft Operations Framework, Program & Project Support Office,

A Level, Information Security Foundation based on ISO/IEC 27002, MCTS (Microsoft SQL Server 2005 Business Intelligence Development),

MCP (Windows 2000 Server), MCTS (SQL Server 2008 Implementation and Maintenance), MCTS (Microsoft Office Project 2007), MCSD (.Net),

MTA (Software Development Fundamentals), MTA (Cloud Fundamentals), MCTS (Configuring - MOSS 2007), MCP (VB6 Distributed), DevOps,

IBM Cloud Computing Architecture, MCP (VB6 Desktop), MCTS (Application Development - MOSS 2007), MCITP (SQL Server 2005),

MCP (Windows 2000 Server), MCTS (Configuring - MOSS 2007), MCTS (BizTalk Server 2006 Custom Applications)

MCTS (.Net Framework 4 Service Communication Applications - Windows Communication Foundation Development)

MCITP (Applications for Microsoft Dynamics CRM, Installation & Configuration for Microsoft Dynamics CRM)

Microsoft Certified Business Management Solution Specialist In Microsoft Dynamics CRM 3.0 Applications

Microsoft Certified Business Management Solution Specialist In Microsoft Dynamics CRM 3.0 Customization

Microsoft Certified Business Management Solution Specialist In Microsoft Dynamics CRM 3.0 Customization

Microsoft Certified Business Management Solution Specialist In Microsoft Dynamics CRM 3.0 Installation and Configuration

Microsoft Certified Business Management Solutions Specialist: Microsoft Dynamics CRM 4.0 Extending Microsoft Dynamics certification

Features of This Book:

- Provides a comprehensive understanding of Large Language Models , including their architecture, evolution, and diverse applications.
- Offers detailed guidance on Pretraining, Fine-tuning, evaluation, and deployment of LLMs.
- Explains instruction Fine-tuning with practical insights into dataset preparation, supervised training, and optimizing for task-specific needs.
- Embeds practical implementation with code examples, best practices, and memory-efficient workflows.
- Highlights evaluation techniques using automated metrics, human preference scoring, and advanced tools like Llama 3.
- Covers scalable assessment methods to streamline large-scale model evaluation effectively.
- Demonstrates real-world applications in customer support, education, creative writing, and technical problem-solving.
- Explores advanced topics like reinforcement learning, hyperparameter tuning, and creating task-specific datasets.
- Maintains a future-oriented perspective by discussing cutting-edge techniques and advancements in AI.
- Caters to both beginners and advanced practitioners, blending foundational knowledge with deep technical expertise.

How to read this Book?

- Start by acknowledging that the book is specifically for individuals to know the Internet of Things concepts.

- Highlight that the book serves as a comprehensive companion for candidates, encompassing a variety of resources such as practice questions, MCQs, and scenarios to learn the basics.

- Determine why you're reading the book. Are you looking to gain a general understanding of IOT, preparing for a course or certification, or aiming to deepen your knowledge in a specific area? Understanding your goals will help you focus your reading.

- While reading, take notes on key concepts, definitions, and explanations. Summarize each chapter or section in your own words to reinforce your understanding.

- Highlight important points or use sticky notes to mark pages for future reference.

- Engage with the material actively by asking questions, solving exercises or problems provided in the book, and experimenting with concepts on your computer if possible. Try to apply what you learn to real-world scenarios to solidify your understanding.

- Supplement your reading with additional resources such as online tutorials, videos, interactive simulations, or academic papers as given in this book. Also do the quiz and exercises.

- Mention that the book includes references, guiding readers to additional resources for further study. This ensures that users can delve deeper into specific topics if needed.

- Periodically review what you've learned to reinforce your understanding and identify any gaps in your knowledge. Reflect on how the concepts you've learned relate to each other and to your overall goals. Consider discussing the material with peers or mentors to gain new insights and perspectives.

How to watch Video?

In our textbook, we have enriched each chapter with a series of YouTube videos, each covering various exercises and aspects of the chapter content. These videos are designed to facilitate a deeper understanding and to aid in exam preparation. To ensure easy access, we provide both direct links and QR codes for each video.

To access these valuable video resources, you may choose one of the two convenient methods outlined below:

1. **Accessing Videos via Direct Link:**

   - **Direct Link Provided:** We have included direct links to the videos within our textbook.
   - **Manual Entry:** You can manually enter the provided link into the browser of your choice on any device, including PCs, tablets, or mobile phones.

2. **Accessing Videos via QR Code:**

   - **Scan QR Code:** For instant access, simply scan the QR Code associated with each video using a QR Code Scanner on your device.
   - **Immediate Playback:** Upon scanning, you'll be directed to the video for immediate viewing.

Note: We have already mentioned how to use QR Code in a separate page, so, if you are facing any issue regarding QR Code Scan, then read How to use QR Codes page. There you can see the steps with images, so you can scan QR code easily.

How to give Online Exam?

To enhance learning and assist in exam preparation, our textbook now include a comprehensive collection of Online Test Paper for each chapter. These interactive exercises cover multiple choice questions, true/false statements, one-word answers, and fill-in-the-blanks, among others, to deepen understanding of the chapter content. For convenient access, you can utilize either direct links or QR Codes provided for each form.

To access these valuable online test papers, you may choose one of the two convenient methods outlined below:

1. **Accessing Online exam via Direct Link:**

   - **Direct Link Provided:** We have included direct links of the Online exam within our textbook.
   - **Manual Entry:** You can manually enter the provided link into the browser of your choice on any device, including PCs, tablets, or mobile phones.

2. **Accessing Online Exam via QR Code:**

   - **Scan QR Code:** For instant access, simply scan the QR Code associated with each Online Test Paper using a QR Code Scanner on your device.
   - **Immediate Playback:** Upon scanning, you'll be directed to the Online exam for immediate viewing.

Top reasons to choose this book

For Teachers

Goal-oriented educational tasks
Forecasting student achievements
Prepared educational resources
Computerised assessment
Supportive digital aide
Evaluation of responses
Sophisticated data analysis
Social media support
24 X 7 IT help desk

For Students

Supportive academic aide
Custom tasks with endless attempts
Prompt responses and clarifications
Customized conversational agents
Motivation through incentive programs
Suggestion engines
Social media support
24 X 7 IT help desk

For Parents

Prompt alerts
Feedback availability on-demand
Instant monitoring of development
Suggested learning materials
Discover educational passions
Social media support
24 X 7 IT help desk

For Institutes

Enhancing student performance
Quick and effective feedback
Continuous growth and learning
Increases efficiency
Advanced planning and strategic insights
Social media support
24 X 7 IT help desk

Key Takeaways

- Large Language Model s (LLMs) are built on transformer architectures, leveraging self-attention mechanisms for context understanding.
- Pretraining on large datasets allows LLMs to acquire general linguistic knowledge and context-aware generation capabilities.
- Fine-tuning adapts pretrained LLMs to specific tasks by using curated datasets and task-specific training objectives.
- Instruction Fine-tuning enhances the ability of LLMs to understand and follow detailed prompts or user queries effectively.
- High-quality instruction-response datasets are critical for training LLMs to generalize across diverse tasks and domains.
- Dynamic padding and efficient batching are essential for optimizing LLM training processes and minimizing computational overhead.
- Model evaluation requires both qualitative and quantitative approaches, including manual inspection and automated scoring systems.
- Metrics like BLEU, ROUGE, and human preference scoring help measure response accuracy and alignment with instructions.
- Tools like automated evaluation using larger LLMs streamline performance assessment across large datasets.
- Reinforcement learning from human feedback (RLHF) can be employed to further refine the instruction-following abilities of LLMs.
- Hyperparameter tuning, including learning rates and batch sizes, plays a significant role in achieving stable and effective training results.
- Using larger pretrained models like GPT-2 Medium improves capacity for nuanced reasoning and complex task performance.
- Response quality can vary depending on the dataset's diversity and relevance to the intended application.
- Limiting sequence lengths ensures that training is compatible with the model's context window and reduces memory usage.
- Saving and reusing fine-tuned models allows for continuity in experimentation and deployment.

- Scalability is a key feature of LLMs, enabling their application in fields like customer support, education, and creative writing.
- Pretrained LLMs often require additional layers of Fine-tuning to address limitations in task-specific scenarios.
- Instruction Fine-tuning transforms LLMs into highly interactive and context-aware tools for real-world applications.
- Advanced evaluation frameworks like AlpacaEval or similar benchmarks enhance reliability in assessing model performance.
- The book emphasizes practical implementation, guiding users through every step of training, Fine-tuning, and deployment.
- Iterative improvements in datasets, training processes, and evaluation methodologies are essential to keep LLMs relevant and effective in evolving use cases.

Table of Content

Chapter 1

EXPLORING LARGE LANGUAGE MODELS

In this chapter you will learn about:

- ☐ Understanding the Basics of LLMs
- ☐ Key Steps in Developing and Applying LLMs
- ☐ Leveraging Extensive Datasets for LLMs
- ☐ Constructing a Large Language Model
- ☐ Practical Uses of Large Language Models
- ☐ An Introduction to Transformer Architecture
- ☐ An In-Depth Look at the GPT Model Structure

ChatGPT and other Large Language Model s (LLMs) (which can be considered as a specialized type of deep neural network model) have revolutionalized Natural Language processing (NLP) over the past couple of years. They represent a huge paradigm shift from traditional NLP methods, which were predominantly rule-based with a lot of hand-coding or very simple models. Traditional NLP techniques were designed for categorization and simpler pattern recognition (e.g., spam filters or document classification) where basic rules or light models do the work well. But their performance on more complex language tasks, which require a nuanced understanding, contextual sensitivity and dynamic generation of coherent text, was not that good. Earlier generations of language models, for example, were not capable of generating an emailbased on a shallow set of keywords or following complex conversational instructions as LLMs can now do pretty easily.

LLMS have dramatically increased the capability to complete complex language tasks, encompassing comprehension, generation and interpretation of human text at a scale and intricacy unseen before. At the same time, just because we are claiming these models "understand" language doesn't mean this "understanding" is comparable to human understanding. LLMs are not conscious, nor do they have a subjective experience: LLMs compute language patterns and provide responses that are plausible-sounding, but deployed without any conceptual framework other than what the model has trained on statistical patterns over large datasets. The evolution of LLMs is made possible through advancements in deep learning, a subcategory of Machine Learning under the general umbrella known as Artificial Intelligence (AI) that utilizes neural networks to handle hierarchical representations with deep architectures composed of multiple layers. The beauty of LLMs lies in the sheer volume of text data they are trained on—from books and articles to online discussions—enabling them to capture much finer contextual details and nuances of human language compared with traditional NLP methods. Due to this massive training, LLMs are capable of performing multiple different NLP tasks such as text translation, sentiment analysis, summarization, question answering and conversational AI, among other things.

One key distinction between modern LLMs and older NLP models is their implementation as general-purpose platforms. Previous NLP models were designed to finalize a specific task (like categorization and sentiment analysis or machine translation) but LLMs are more generalisable for all language functions without re-training each function. LLMs are powerful and generalisable across a wide range of domains, from automating scalable customer service work to content generation and even in more technical fields like code generation or data analysis. Two main components have resulted in the astonishing capabilities for Large Language Model s : the transformer architecture and massive datasets for Pretraining these architectures. The transformer architecture, discovered in 2017 by researchers at Google, overcame many of the limitations imposed by earlier architectures, such as poorly supported parallelisation and the long-range dependencies tracked within text — features that recurrent neural networks (RNNs) could not address as they were predominantly sequential. It is this paradigmatic nature of transformers that enables them to capture not only the syntax and semantics but even vast amounts of it and culturally nuanced linguistic patterns, given their ability to pay attention to multiple layers over different parts of a text simultaneously. Together with big datasets, transformers allow the LLMs to encode a wide range of language characteristics and context that would be impossible to engineer or capture in simpler models manually.

That movement of transformer-based models in combination with large training datasets has led to a paradigm shift to NLP, providing tools that are much better summarised, generated and communicated by human language. As such, in this book, we intend to establish the basis of how LLMs work via understanding the principles behind transformers and what it takes to train them. In this, readers will build a ChatGPT-like LLM in transformer architecture from scratch, following a step-by-step approach to understanding both practical and theoretical knowledge behind such models so they can replicate and add further developments on their own.

1.1 Understanding the Basics of LLMs

A Large Language Model (LLM) is an extensive neural network trained to comprehend, produce and respond with human-like text. These models, which are essentially deep neural networks that learn on a massive corpus of text data (usually large scale datasets containing anything publicly available on the internet), Such training allows LLMs to learn complex linguistic patterns, contextual information, and a subtle understanding of human language.

Large refers to both the colossal datasets used for training and the large number of parameters in the model. These modern LLMs, such as OpenAI's GPT-4, Google's PaLM and Meta's LLaMA contain tens or even hundreds of billions or parameters. These parameters are tunable weights in the neural network that are trained (or tuned) to maximise its ability to correctly predict what the next word will be given all prior words in a sentence. Next word prediction sounds simple, but it takes advantage of the time sequence property of language and allows the model to learn complicated context, grammar, and inter-text relationships. The surprising depth of understanding and versatility achieved by models trained through this deceptively simple task continues to astonish researchers. We will discuss and implement the next, in subsequent chapters.

LLMs are powered by transformer architecture, a ground breaking design that enables models to focus on relevant parts of an input sequence when making predictions. Transformers use "attention mechanisms" to weigh different words or phrases based on their relevance, making them exceptionally effective at managing the complexities of human language, including long-range dependencies, intricate sentence structures, and nuanced context. Due to their ability to generate coherent, contextually relevant responses, LLMs fall under the category of generative Artificial Intelligence, often abbreviated as generative AI or GenAI. In the broader field of Artificial Intelligence (AI), generative models play a key role in creating content that mirrors human-like understanding and production, including language, images, and even complex decision-making tasks. AI itself is a broad field encompassing Machine Learning , deep learning, and other methodologies, such as symbolic reasoning, rule-based systems, genetic algorithms, and expert systems.

Historically, tasks like spam classification relied on traditional Machine Learning techniques where human experts manually extracted features. For example, email classifiers might look for keywords (like "prize" or "win"), capital letters, excessive punctuation, or suspicious links, all of which require careful curation by experts. Deep learning, however, allows models to learn relevant features directly from data, without manual feature selection. While both traditional Machine Learning and deep learning approaches still require labelled data (such as identifying emails as spam or not), deep learning models benefit from automatically extracting complex patterns that may not be obvious to human observers.

Today, LLMs are applied to a wide range of tasks beyond basic text classification, including complex problem-solving, creative writing, code generation, interactive dialogue, and more. They have transformed fields such as customer support, content creation, language translation, and even specialised areas like healthcare, where they assist in clinical documentation and medical research. The versatility of LLMs comes from their capacity to generalise across many different types of language tasks, unlike earlier models that were typically limited to narrow applications. The success of LLMs is primarily due to the transformer architecture and access to vast datasets, which enable them to learn from a wide variety of linguistic nuances and patterns that would be challenging to encode manually. This shift to transformer-based models, combined with large-scale training, has revolutionised NLP by providing tools that are capable of interpreting and generating human language with impressive accuracy and adaptability.

In this book, we will explore the fundamental components of LLMs, culminating in the step-by-step implementation of an LLM similar to ChatGPT. This hands-on approach will provide a deep understanding of the architecture and processes involved in creating a powerful language model, from the fundamentals of neural networks to the intricacies of transformer layers and attention mechanisms.

1.2 Practical Uses of Large Language Models

Due to their advanced abilities to analyse and comprehend unstructured text, Large Language Model s (LLMs) have become indispensable across a multitude of fields. Today, LLMs are employed in diverse applications, including machine translation, text generation, sentiment analysis, summarisation, and many others. They have proven highly effective in content creation, from generating fiction and articles to assisting with programming tasks. LLMs also power sophisticated virtual assistants and chatbots, like OpenAI's ChatGPT and Google's Gemini (previously Bard), which are capable of understanding complex queries, holding conversations, and enhancing traditional search experiences in platforms like Google Search and Microsoft, Bing. These models bring an intuitive, conversational layer to search engines, providing more interactive and context-aware responses to user questions.

In specialised domains such as healthcare, law, and academia, LLMs facilitate efficient information retrieval from extensive databases and can assist in tasks like document analysis, summarisation, and answering complex, field-specific questions. For example, they are being used to help medical professionals sift through clinical documentation or legal researchers analyse case law more effectively.

LLMs are transforming the way we interact with text by automating tasks that require deep understanding and generation of language. Their potential applications are vast, and as technology evolves, LLMs are poised to make technology more conversational, accessible, and user-friendly in our daily lives. We will build an understanding of LLMs from the ground up, constructing a model capable of generating text. You'll learn about the techniques that enable LLMs to handle a wide range of tasks, including answering questions, summarizing information, translating text, and more. Through this hands-on approach, you'll gain insights into how advanced AI systems like ChatGPT function by creating your own model step by step.

1.3 Key Steps in Developing and Applying LLMs

Building your own LLM provides a valuable learning experience, enabling a deep understanding of its inner workings, strengths, and limitations. This hands-on approach equips you with the skills needed to pretrain or fine-tune existing open- source LLMs, tailoring them to specific domains or tasks. Custom-built LLMs, optimized for specialised applications, can often outperform general-purpose models like ChatGPT, which are designed to cover a broad spectrum of tasks. Industry- specific LLMs, such as BloombergGPT for finance or models crafted for medical question-answering, illustrate the potential of targeted customization. By developing models specifically aligned with a domain's unique language and requirements, you can achieve higher performance in specialized tasks.

Moreover, creating custom LLMs has significant advantages in terms of data privacy and control. Companies with sensitive data may prefer to avoid sharing it with external LLM providers like OpenAI, and custom models can be deployed locally on devices such as laptops and smartphones, minimizing reliance on external servers. This approach reduces latency, decreases server costs, and enables companies to maintain complete control over model updates and adaptations. Apple, for example, is actively exploring the potential of deploying smaller, efficient LLMs directly on user devices.

Building an LLM generally involves two stages: Pretraining and Fine-tuning. Pretraining is the initial phase, where the model is trained on a large, diverse dataset to develop a foundational understanding of language. This broad understanding serves as a basis for further refinement. In the Fine-tuning phase, the model is trained on a narrower, domain-specific dataset to optimize performance for particular tasks or industries.

This two-stage training approach allows the model to adapt from general language understanding to specialised applications.

Pretraining begins by training the model on a vast corpus of text data, often referred to as "raw text" because it lacks labelled information. Although filtering may be applied to remove irrelevant characters or unknown languages, the data itself is usually unstructured. Unlike traditional Machine Learning methods, which rely on labelled data, the Pretraining phase of LLMs employs self-supervised learning, where the model generates its own labels from the data by predicting the next word in a sequence. This process allows the model to learn context, syntax, and semantics without manual annotation. Once the LLM is pretrained, a base or foundation model can be created, and further training can be conducted through Fine-tuning. Fine-tuning involves training the model on labelled data to enhance its performance for specific tasks. Two common types of Fine-tuning are instruction Fine-tuning and classification Fine-tuning. In instruction Fine-tuning, the dataset consists of pairs of instructions and responses, such as translation requests with their correct translations. In classification Fine-tuning, the dataset includes text and associated class labels, such as emails labelled as "spam" or "not spam."

This book will guide you through coding implementations for both Pretraining and Fine-tuning an LLM. We will cover the technical details of creating a base LLM, as well as delve into instruction and classification Fine-tuning, providing you with the knowledge to build and customize LLMs for a variety of applications.

1.4 An Introduction to Transformer Architecture

Most modern Large Language Model s (LLMs) are built on the transformer architecture, a deep neural network architecture introduced in the influential 2017 paper, *"Attention Is All You Need."* Initially developed for machine translation tasks, such as translating English texts into German and French, the transformer architecture has since become the foundation of a wide array of NLP applications.

The transformer consists of two main components: an Encoder and a Decoder. The Encoder processes the input text and transforms it into a series of numerical representations, or vectors, that capture the contextual nuances of the input. In a typical translation task, the Encoder takes the text from the source language, encodes it into vectors, and passes these representations to the Decoder. The Decoder then uses these vectors to generate text in the target language. Both the Encoder and Decoder are built with multiple layers interconnected by a self-attention mechanism, a key feature that enables transformers to handle complex language tasks effectively.

A crucial element of transformers and LLMs in general is the self-attention mechanism, which allows the model to weigh the relevance of different words or tokens in a sequence relative to each other. This mechanism captures long-range dependencies and contextual relationships within the input, greatly enhancing the model's ability to produce coherent and contextually relevant responses. Due to its importance, we will explore the self-attention mechanism in detail in later chapters, implementing it step by step to understand its inner workings.

Since the original transformer, numerous specialised models have been developed, expanding on its Encoder-Decoder architecture to optimise performance for different tasks. Notable among these are BERT (Bidirectional Encoder Representations from Transformers) and the GPT (Generative Pretrained Transformer) family of models. BERT builds upon the Encoder component of the transformer and is particularly suited for text classification tasks, such as sentiment analysis and document categorisation. It uses a masked language model training approach, where the model predicts hidden words within a sentence. This training strategy makes BERT highly effective at understanding text context and is used by platforms like X (formerly Twitter) to detect toxic content.

GPT models, in contrast, focus on the Decoder portion of the transformer architecture and are designed for generative tasks, including text completion, summarisation, machine translation, creative writing, and code generation. The GPT family, from GPT-2 and GPT-3 to the more recent GPT-4, has demonstrated remarkable versatility, showcasing an ability to handle a broad range of tasks without task-specific training. A key strength of GPT models lies in their proficiency with zero-shot and few- shot learning. Zero shot learning allows the model to generalise to tasks it hasn't specifically been trained for, handling new tasks with no prior examples. Few-shot learning, on the other hand, enables the model to perform tasks with only a few provided examples, effectively adapting to the task based on minimal input.

The transformer architecture, the powerful Encoder-Decoder structure, and the self-attention mechanism have made LLMs an essential technology for Natural Language understanding and generation. In the following chapters, we will dive deeper into the principles behind transformers, exploring the Encoder, Decoder, and self-attention mechanisms in detail and learning how to implement them step by step to build a foundational understanding of LLMs.

Transformers VS Large Language Model s (LLMs)

Aspect	**Transformers**	**Large Language Models (LLMs)**
Definition	A deep neural network architecture introduced primarily for language tasks, but now used in various fields, including computer vision.	A type of model designed to understand, generate, and respond to human-like text.
Relationship	Transformers form the basis of most modern LLMs, particularly those focused on language tasks.	Most LLMs today are based on transformer architecture, although alternative architectures also exist.
Alternative Architectures	Transformers are commonly used for non-language tasks, such as computer vision.	Some LLMs are based on recurrent or convolutional architectures, aimed at improving computational efficiency.
Terminology	Not all transformers are LLMs, as they can serve non-language tasks.	In common usage, "LLM" usually refers to transformer-based models like GPT, but the term may include models based on other architectures.
Computational Efficiency	Transformer-based models, especially for LLMs, require significant computational resources.	Alternative architectures are being explored to make LLMs more efficient, though they're not yet as widely adopted as transformer-based LLMs.
Adoption in Practice	Transformer-based architectures are widely used across various fields.	Alternative LLM architectures are still emerging; it is unclear if they will become as widely used as transformer-based LLMs.

1.5 Leveraging Extensive Datasets for LLMs

The remarkable capabilities of Large Language Model s (LLMs), such as GPT-4, LLaMA, and PaLM, largely stem from their training on extensive datasets. These models rely on massive volumes of data to learn complex language patterns, contexts, and nuanced meanings, which enable them to handle a variety of tasks, perform in-context learning, and exhibit emergent abilities that were not explicitly programmed. The datasets used in training LLMs are diverse, ranging from general internet text to highly specialised domain-specific content. Public internet data provides a vast array of information from websites, articles, books, and forums, ensuring models are exposed to different language styles and subject areas. Additionally, scientific and academic literature, sourced from collections like PubMed and ArXiv, offers models exposure to technical language and detailed explanations, strengthening their performance in specialised fields such as medicine and computer science. News datasets keep the models updated on recent events, allowing them to generate summaries or analyses that are timely and relevant. Domain-specific data is another crucial component, as some LLMs are fine-tuned on specialised datasets to optimise performance for particular industries. For instance, BloombergGPT, trained on financial data, is tailored to tasks in finance, while models focused on healthcare or legal fields gain proficiency through exposure to clinical or legal texts.

Two critical factors in dataset effectiveness are the size and diversity of the data. Larger datasets provide extensive examples, enabling the model to capture rare words, unique phrases, and complex relationships that smaller datasets might miss. The diversity of datasets ensures that the model can generalise well across tasks, handling everything from casual conversation to technical writing with accuracy. Models like GPT-4 likely involve multilingual data, allowing them to perform well in multiple languages and cultural contexts. Curating extensive datasets presents both challenges and advancements. Synthetic data generation has become a valuable technique, creating additional training data to complement real-world examples. This approach introduces variations the model might not encounter otherwise, helping it become more robust. Human feedback also plays a critical role in refining dataset quality, often through methods like Reinforcement Learning from Human Feedback (RLHF), which aligns model output with human expectations. Quality control measures, such as filtering to remove spam, duplicates, and inappropriate content, ensure that the dataset enhances the model's knowledge while minimising biases and inaccuracies.

While large datasets are essential for training, they bring challenges and ethical considerations. Privacy is a significant concern, as LLMs trained on extensive datasets may inadvertently learn sensitive information. Techniques such as differential privacy, data anonymisation, and filtering help prevent models from retaining specific details, thereby protecting privacy. Additionally, because internet data often contains biases, developers are actively working to identify and mitigate these biases to ensure balanced and fair model responses. Companies like Google and Meta are exploring ways to reduce the environmental footprint by optimising data usage and hardware efficiency.

Dataset	Quantity (tokens)	Weight in training mix	Epochs elapsed when training for 300B tokens
Common Crawl (filtered)	410 billion	60%	0.44
WebText2	19 billion	22%	2.9
Books1	12 billion	8%	1.9
Books2	55 billion	8%	0.43
Wikipedia	3 billion	3%	3.4

Table for Dataset of GPT - 3

Recent models showcase the benefits of extensive datasets in practice. GPT-4, for example, was trained on a vast and diverse dataset, enabling it to perform tasks across various languages and handle complex queries, from technical insights to legal interpretations. Meta's LLaMA models aim to balance dataset quality with model efficiency, achieving strong performance on benchmarks while keeping model size manageable. Anthropic's Claude models, designed with an emphasis on alignment and safety, use RLHF and careful filtering to ensure the model's responses align with ethical standards. Bloomberg GPT, trained on financial datasets, exemplifies the advantages of domain-specific data, excelling at analysing financial reports and interpreting market trends.

Looking ahead, future LLMs may adopt adaptive data selection, allowing models to continually learn from new, relevant information without needing to be retrained from scratch. Federated learning is another promising approach, which allows models to train across decentralised devices without centralising data, enhancing user privacy. Real-world interaction data may also play a role in future models, enabling continuous improvement based on direct user feedback and making LLMs even more adaptable and responsive. In summary, leveraging extensive datasets has become the foundation of powerful, versatile LLMs. While challenges in data quality, privacy, and ethics are significant, addressing them will be crucial for the responsible development of future LLMs.

1.6 An In-Depth Look at the GPT Model Structure

The GPT model was first introduced in OpenAI's paper, *"Improving Language Understanding by Generative Pre-Training"* by Radford et al. GPT-3, a more advanced version, scaled up the original model with a significantly larger number of parameters and a more extensive training dataset. The initial model in ChatGPT was created by Fine-tuning GPT-3 on a large dataset of instructional data, employing a method outlined in OpenAI's Instruct GPT research. This Fine-tuning enabled the model to excel not only at text completion but also at a variety of tasks, such as spelling correction, classification, and language translation. The impressive versatility of GPT models comes from their Pretraining on a simple yet powerful next-word prediction task.

Next-word prediction is a form of self-supervised learning, where the model learns to predict the next word in a sentence based on the preceding words. This self-labelling approach doesn't require explicitly labelled data; instead, the structure of the text itself serves as the label. By using each subsequent word as a label, the model can be trained on massive, unlabeled text datasets, making it feasible to create large-scale language models without needing extensive manual annotation. Compared to the original transformer, which consists of both an Encoder and a Decoder, GPT uses only the Decoder component. This design makes GPT an auto-regressive model, generating each word sequentially based on the preceding sequence. By training the model to predict each word in context, GPT develops an understanding of language patterns and structure, resulting in coherent and contextually relevant text generation.

GPT-3, introduced in 2020, marked a milestone with its 96 transformer layers and a staggering 175 billion parameters, making it one of the largest language models of its time. Despite newer architectures like Meta's LLaMA models, which introduce minor refinements, the foundational principles behind GPT remain relevant. Understanding GPT's architecture, with its focus on Decoder-only, autoregressive generation, provides essential insights into the operation of many modern LLMs, which often incorporate slight adjustments to this core design. The GPT architecture, initially aimed at next-word prediction, has shown capabilities beyond its intended design, including tasks like language translation. This phenomenon, where models perform tasks they were not explicitly trained for, is known as emergent behavior. Emergent behaviors arise naturally as a result of the model's exposure to vast and diverse datasets, often including multilingual data. This exposure enables GPT models to identify translation patterns between languages and apply them effectively, despite having no specific training for translation. The ability to generalize to new tasks underscores the power of large-scale generative models and highlights the unexpected advantages of extensive Pretraining on diverse data.

1.7 Constructing a Large Language Model

With a solid understanding of Large Language Model s (LLMs) established, it's time to dive into building one from scratch. Using the core concepts behind GPT as our framework, we'll approach this project in three stages.

In the first stage, we'll cover essential data preprocessing steps and implement the attention mechanism-the core of all LLMs. This stage will provide a foundational understanding of how attention enables models to weigh different parts of an input sequence, improving comprehension and generation abilities.

In the second stage, we'll code and pretrain a GPT-inspired LLM that can generate new text. This stage will introduce you to the key principles of Pretraining, where the model learns language structure and patterns through a next-word prediction task. While Pretraining large-scale models from scratch typically require substantial computing resources, our focus here will be on a smaller dataset and model size for educational purposes. We'll also explore how to load publicly available model weights, allowing you to build on existing pretrained models without the need for extensive computational resources.

Finally, in the third stage, we'll take a pretrained LLM and fine-tune it to perform specific tasks like answering questions or classifying text—some of the most common real-world applications of LLMs. Fine-tuning allows us to adapt the model to specialised tasks by training on smaller, task-specific datasets, transforming a general-purpose model into one capable of more targeted performance.

This journey into building and Fine-tuning an LLM will provide you with a deep, practical understanding of how these models work and how to adapt them for various applications. Let's get started!

SUMMARY

✓ Large Language Model s (LLMs) like ChatGPT have transformed NLP by moving away from rule-based methods to deep learning-based approaches that handle complex tasks, including conversational AI and text generation.

✓ LLMs achieve a high degree of language understanding through training on massive datasets, enabling them to handle tasks such as translation, sentiment analysis, summarisation, and more.

✓ Unlike previous models designed for specific tasks, LLMs are general-purpose and can be adapted across a variety of domains, making them highly versatile.

✓ The transformer architecture, with its self-attention mechanism, is the foundation of LLMs, enabling them to manage long-range dependencies and contextual relationships within text.

✓ The power of transformers, combined with access to vast datasets, has made LLMs exceptionally proficient at generating human-like responses and performing advanced language tasks.

✓ Building a custom LLM allows for specialised performance in certain industries and applications, enhancing both privacy and control for organizations.

✓ Training LLMs involves a two-stage process of Pretraining on large datasets followed by Fine-tuning on specialised data, allowing models to adapt to specific tasks or fields.

✓ LLMs are trained using self-supervised learning, where models generate labels from the data itself, enabling large-scale training without manual annotation.

✓ GPT models, based on a Decoder-only transformer architecture, use next-word prediction to build coherent and contextually relevant language generation capabilities, even handling tasks like translation.

✓ Building an LLM involves understanding data preprocessing, implementing attention mechanisms, and Fine-tuning, enabling readers to create adaptable and powerful language models.

Exercises

Exercise 1 – Multiple Choice Questions

1. What is the primary purpose of an LLM?

   A) To perform basic arithmetic

   B) To understand and generate human-like text

   C) To organize files

   D) To execute code directly

2. Which architecture is commonly used for training modern LLMs?

   A) Convolutional Neural Networks B) Recurrent Neural Networks

   C) Transformer D) Support Vector Machine

Exercise 2 – One Word Answers

1. What term is used for the neural network layer that helps LLMs focus on relevant parts of the input sequence?
2. What is the initial phase of training an LLM, where it learns basic language patterns from a large corpus of text?

Exercise 3 – Small Answers

1. Why is the transformer architecture widely used in LLMs?
2. What is the difference between Pretraining and Fine-tuning in LLMs?

Exercise 4 – Long Answers

1. Explain the significance of self-supervised learning in the Pretraining of LLMs.
2. Describe how Fine-tuning can adapt an LLM for a specialized application, providing an example.

Answer

Exercise 1 – 1) B, 2) C

Exercise 2 – 1) Attention, 2) Pretraining

Online Resources

	Practice Paper	YouTube Video Playlist Link
Link	https://forms.gle/KnAZwiW3FvPXDp9B8	https://www.youtube.com/playlist?list=PLzlh_31VWEFoCv8A0fBY2xgxterPZzpep
QR Code		

Chapter 2

WORKING WITH TEXTUAL DATA

In this chapter you will learn about:

- Grasping Word Embeddings
- Breaking Down Text into Tokens
- Mapping Tokens to Token IDs
- Adding Context-Specific Tokens
- Implementing Byte Pair Encoding
- Sampling Data with a Sliding Window Technique
- Creating Embeddings for Tokens

So far, we've explored the overall framework of Large Language Model s (LLMs) and discussed their Pretraining on extensive text datasets. We focused specifically on Decoder-only LLMs, which rely on transformer architecture—an approach foundational to models like ChatGPT and other GPT-based LLMs. During Pretraining, LLMs analyze text sequentially, predicting one word at a time. They achieve remarkable language capabilities by training these models with millions or even billions of parameters on a next-word prediction task. These pre-trained models can then be fine-tuned to follow broad instructions or perform specialized tasks. However, preparing the dataset is essential before implementing and training LLMs.

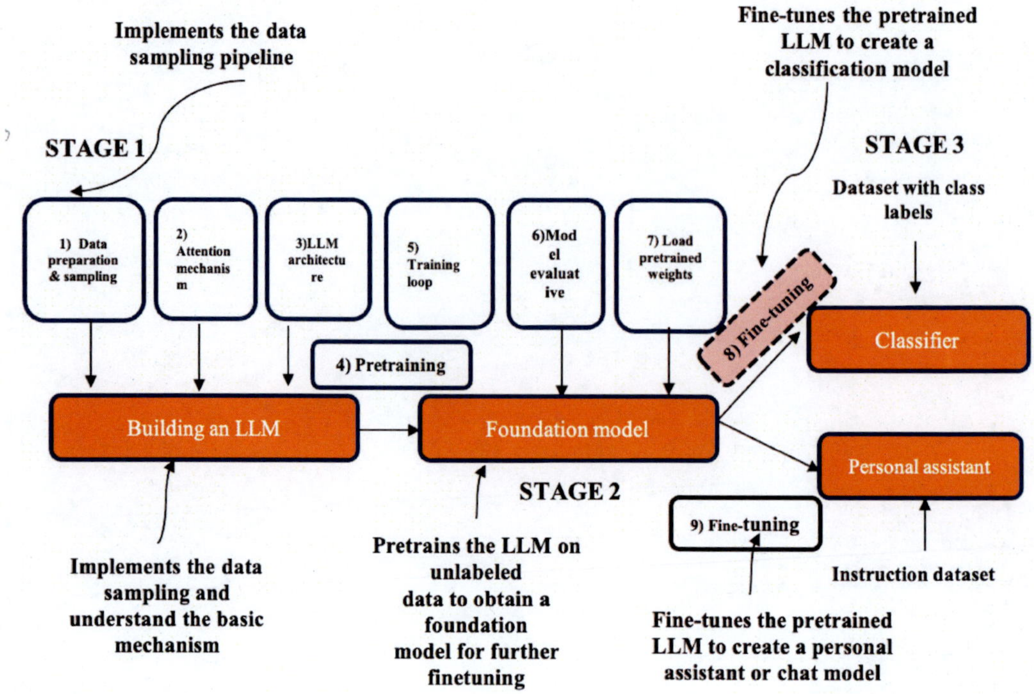

You'll learn to preprocess input text, which involves dividing it into tokens, including words and subwords, to be encoded into vector formats suitable for LLMs. This process often utilises advanced tokenisation methods like byte pair encoding, which is widely used in prominent LLMs such as GPT. Additionally, you'll implement a sampling and data-loading strategy to generate the input-output pairs needed for effective LLM training.

2.1 Grasping Word Embeddings

Deep neural network models, including Large Language Model s (LLMs) like GPT-4, cannot process raw text directly. Since text is categorical, it needs to be represented in a continuous numerical format to enable the mathematical operations essential for neural networks. This process is known as embedding, where words, sentences, or even entire documents are converted into vectorised representations that neural networks can process.

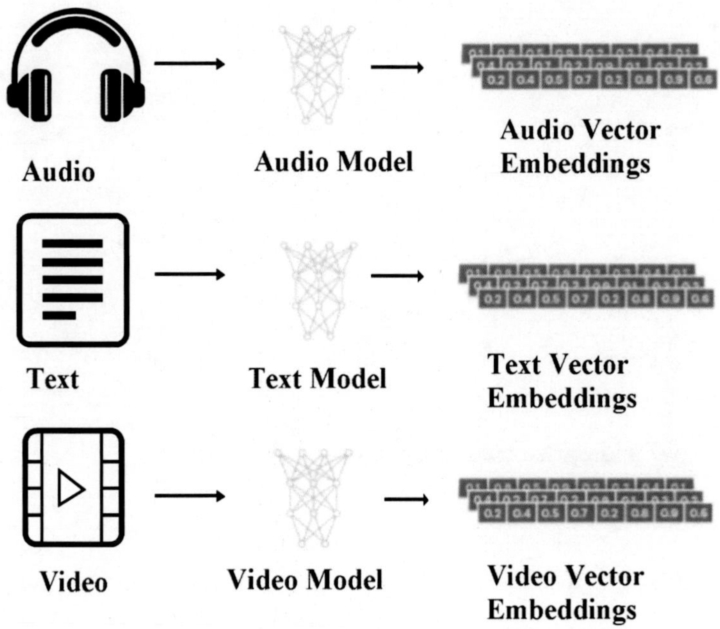

Embeddings, produced by specialised neural network layers or pretrained models, transform discrete data—like text, images, or audio—into points in a continuous vector space. Different data types, however, require distinct embedding models. For instance, a model optimised for text would not suit video or audio embeddings. Text embeddings typically begin with word embeddings, although sentence, paragraph, or document embeddings also exist for tasks requiring broader context, like retrieval-augmented generation (RAG). RAG integrates text generation with information retrieval to improve relevance when generating responses, a technique that has become popular in models like GPT-4.

Several methods for generating word embeddings exist, with Word2Vec being a foundational approach. Word2Vec builds embeddings by training a neural network to predict a word's context based on its neighbouring words. This method demonstrates that words appearing in similar contexts generally have related meanings. High-dimensional word embeddings allow models to capture more nuanced relationships between terms, albeit with increased computational demands. Embedding dimensions can range from tens to thousands depending on the complexity of the task and the model; for example, GPT-4 employs embedding sizes adapted to its extensive architecture to balance performance and efficiency.

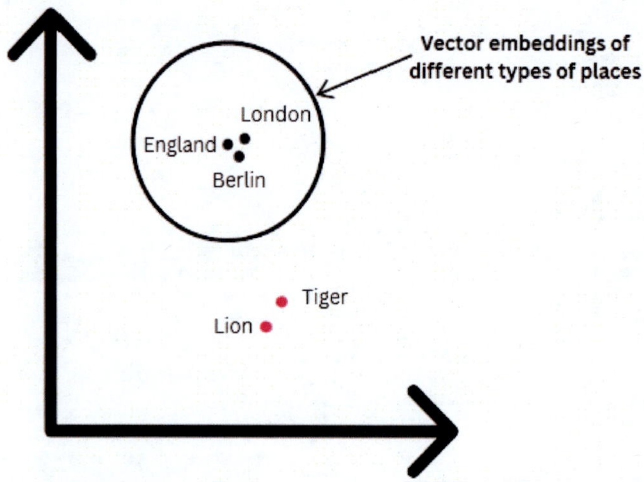

If word embeddings are two-dimensional, we can plot them in a two dimensional scatterplot for visualization purposes as shown here. When using word embedding techniques, such as Word2Vec, words corresponding to similar concepts often appear close to each other in the embedding space. For instance, different types of places appear closer to each other in the embedding space than animals.

While pretrained embeddings like Word2Vec are useful, LLMs like GPT-4 often generate embeddings internally. These embeddings are optimised as part of the training process, allowing the model to develop representations specific to its training data and objectives. This Fine-tuning enables the model to produce contextualised output embeddings that dynamically adjust based on input context.

High-dimensional embeddings, like those used in GPT-4, present visualisation challenges since typical visualisation tools are limited to two or three dimensions. Nevertheless, these complex embeddings play a crucial role in achieving the model's performance, as they capture intricate relationships across vast amounts of data.

2.2 Breaking Down Text into Tokens

To understand how LLMs work with language data, we need to transform the raw text into a form the model can interpret. This process is called tokenisation, and it's essential for breaking down text into smaller parts, or tokens, that are more manageable for the model to process. In modern language models like GPT-4, tokenisation allows the model to effectively capture the text's meaning, context, and structure. Let's explore this process in depth, including recent methods, code examples, and sample outputs.

Tokenisation is the process of splitting text into smaller units, such as words, characters, or subwords. In Natural Language processing (NLP), tokenisation helps transform language data from a continuous sequence of characters into discrete elements that neural networks can process.

1. **Word Tokenisation:** Splits text into individual words. This is a traditional approach, but can struggle with complex language structures, misspellings, or non-standard vocabulary.
2. **Subword Tokenisation:** Breaks down text into parts of words, making it ideal for handling unknown or rare words by combining smaller, known units.
3. **Character Tokenisation:** Breaks text down into individual characters. Though computationally expensive, it's useful in cases requiring a high degree of language flexibility.

   Most recent LLMs, like GPT-4, use subword tokenisation because it balances capturing word meaning and flexibility with language.

Tokenisation Approaches in Modern LLMs

1. **Byte-Pair Encoding (BPE):** An iterative algorithm that merges the most frequent character pairs in the text, creating new "subwords" until a vocabulary size is reached. This approach is widely used in models like GPT-2 and GPT-3.
2. **Unigram Language Model:** An algorithm that builds a probabilistic model of subwords to retain the most meaningful subword pieces. It is particularly useful for handling multilingual data.
3. **SentencePiece:** Developed by Google, this approach uses both BPE and Unigram models to tokenize text without whitespace, making it useful for languages where words are not clearly separated by spaces.
4. **WordPiece:** Similar to BPE but uses likelihood-based merging, which is a technique employed in models like BERT.

   Each approach has its strengths, and the choice of tokenization method can impact the model's performance and efficiency.

   Using Python, we can explore tokenization with popular libraries like `transformers` from Hugging Face and `sentencepiece`. Let's start with an example using Hugging Face's `GPT-2` tokenizer, which is based on BPE.

Step 1: Installing Libraries

If you haven't already, install the `Transformers` library:

```
!pip install transformers
```

Step 2: Tokenizing Text

Let's load a tokenizer, use it on a sample text, and review the outputs.

```
from transformers import GPT2Tokenizer

# Initialize the tokenizer

tokenizer = GPT2Tokenizer.from_pretrained("gpt2")

# Sample text

text = "The Verdict by Edith Wharton is an engaging story that explores human relationships."

# Tokenize the text

tokens = tokenizer.tokenize(text)

token_ids = tokenizer.encode(text)

# Output the tokens and their corresponding IDs

print("Tokens:", tokens)

print("Token IDs:", token_ids)
```

Expected Output:

Tokens: ['The', 'ĠVerdict', 'Ġby', 'ĠEdith', 'ĠWharton', 'Ġis', 'Ġan', 'Ġengaging', 'Ġstory', 'Ġthat', 'Ġexplores', 'Ġhuman', 'Ġrelationships', '.']

Token IDs: [464, 10634, 345, 23009, 10657, 318, 281, 3812, 10227, 326, 9722, 1106, 6779, 13]

In this example:

- The tokeniser has split the sentence into subwords (indicated by Ġ), punctuation, and words. Notice how "The Verdict" and "by Edith Wharton" are tokenised into unique units instead of individual characters.
- Each token is mapped to a specific integer ID representing it in the model's vocabulary.

Explanation of Output:

- **Tokens:** Each word or subword is represented as a token, allowing the model to process words that may be unknown or rare.
- **Token IDs:** Each token is converted into an ID, creating a sequence that the LLM uses for processing.

  This encoding enables the model to read, process, and make predictions based on the tokenised input.

  Handling Tokenization Output in LLMs

  In models like GPT-4, the tokenised IDs (as shown in token_ids above) are fed as input for processing. The LLM then uses these IDs to create embeddings, which are high-dimensional vector representations of each token.

  Choosing Tokenization Parameters for LLM Training

1. **Vocabulary Size:** Determines the variety of tokens the model can represent. Larger vocabularies provide more granularity but increase computational complexity.
2. **Subword Units:** Define how words are broken down, balancing the preservation of full words and the allowance of flexible combinations.
3. **Max Sequence Length:** Specifies the maximum number of tokens processed at once. If a sentence exceeds this length, then it may be truncated or split into separate segments.

2.3 Mapping Tokens to Token IDs

To convert tokens into integer representations, which we call token IDs, we first need to build a vocabulary. This vocabulary maps each unique word and special character to a unique integer, allowing the model to interpret text in a numerical form.

Assuming we have already tokenised The Verdict by Edith Wharton and stored the tokens in a Python variable called preprocessed, let's create a list of all unique tokens, sort them alphabetically, and determine the vocabulary size.

Here's how to create the vocabulary:

```
# Get unique tokens and sort them

all_words = sorted(set(preprocessed))

vocab_size = len(all_words)

print("Vocabulary size:", vocab_size)
```

After running this code, we determine that the vocabulary size is 1,130. Now, let's assign each unique token a unique integer ID.

Creating a Vocabulary:

The following code builds a dictionary that maps each token to a unique integer, which we'll use to convert text into token IDs:

```
# Create a vocabulary mapping each token to an integer
vocab = {token: integer for integer, token in enumerate(all_words)}
# Display the first 51 entries for illustration
for i, item in enumerate(vocab.items()):
    print(item)
    if i >= 50:
        break
```

Sample Output:

```
('!', 0)
('"', 1)
("'", 2)
...
('Her', 49)
('Hermia', 50)
```

In this dictionary, each unique token is assigned an integer ID, establishing a standardised way to represent words and symbols. With the vocabulary defined, we can now convert any new text into token IDs by looking up each token in the vocabulary and substituting it with its corresponding integer. This numeric format is essential for further steps like embedding creation, where each token ID will be transformed into a high-dimensional vector suitable for model processing.

Let's implement a tokeniser class in Python, Simple TokenizerV1, that includes methods for encoding (converting text to token IDs) and decoding (converting token IDs back to text). This class will use a given vocabulary to map each token to a unique integer and handle the reverse mapping as well. We'll then test this tokeniser on sample text, covering both successful cases and scenarios where the vocabulary lacks certain words.

Implementing a simple text tokeniser

```
import re

class SimpleTokenizerV1:

    def __init__(self, vocab):

        """

        Initializes the tokenizer with a given vocabulary.

        Creates mappings for string-to-integer and integer-to-string conversions.

        :param vocab: Dictionary mapping tokens (strings) to unique integer IDs

        """

        self.str_to_int = vocab  # Map from token string to unique integer ID
        self.int_to_str = {i: s for s, i in vocab.items()}  # Reverse map for decoding
    def encode(self, text):
        """

        Encodes the input text into a sequence of token IDs based on the vocabulary.
        :param text: Input text to be tokenized and encoded
        :return: List of token IDs corresponding to the text
        """

        # Tokenize the text by splitting on punctuation and whitespace
        preprocessed = re.split(r'([,.?_!"()\']|--|\s)', text)
        # Remove empty strings and strip whitespace from tokens
        preprocessed = [item.strip() for item in preprocessed if item.strip()]
        # Map each token to its corresponding integer ID using the vocabulary
        ids = [self.str_to_int[s] for s in preprocessed if s in self.str_to_int]
        return ids
    def decode(self, ids):
        """

        Decodes a sequence of token IDs back into the original text.
        :param ids: List of token IDs to be converted back to text
        :return: Decoded text as a string
        """

        # Map each integer ID back to its string token
        text = " ".join([self.int_to_str[i] for i in ids])
        # Remove unnecessary spaces around punctuation
        text = re.sub(r'\s+([,.?!"()\'])', r'\1', text)
        return text
```

```
# Sample Vocabulary for Tokenization
vocab = {
    '"': 1, 'It': 56, "'": 2, 's': 850, 'the': 988, 'last': 602,
    'he': 533, 'painted': 746, 'you': 5, 'know': 1126, 'Mrs.': 596,
    'Gisburn': 67, 'said': 7, 'with': 38, 'pardonable': 851, 'pride': 1108
}
# Instantiate the tokenizer with the vocabulary
tokenizer = SimpleTokenizerV1(vocab)
# Text to Encode
text = """"It's the last he painted, you know," Mrs. Gisburn said with pardonable pride."""
# Encode the text into token IDs
ids = tokenizer.encode(text)
print("Encoded Token IDs:", ids)
# Decode the token IDs back into text
decoded_text = tokenizer.decode(ids)
print("Decoded Text:", decoded_text)
# Test the tokeniser on text with unknown words
new_text = "Hello, do you like tea?"
try:
    # Attempt to encode text with unknown words
    new_ids = tokenizer.encode(new_text)
    print("Encoded Token IDs for New Text:", new_ids)
except KeyError as e:
    print(f"Encoding error: The word '{e.args[0]}' is not in the vocabulary.")
```

Sample Output

Encoded Token IDs: [1, 56, 2, 850, 988, 602, 533, 746, 5, 1126, 596, 5, 1, 67, 7, 38, 851, 1108, 754, 793, 7]

Decoded Text: " It's the last he painted, you know," Mrs. Gisburn said with pardonable pride.

Encoding error: The word 'Hello' is not in the vocabulary.

Explanation of the Code

__init__ Method:

Initializes the tokenizer with a given vocabulary.
Sets up two dictionaries: str_to_int for mapping tokens to IDs and int_to_str for the reverse mapping.

encode Method:

Takes input text, splits it using regular expressions to handle punctuation and whitespace, and removes any empty tokens.

Maps each token to its integer ID based on the vocabulary.
If a token is missing in the vocabulary, it can cause a KeyError, which we handle in testing.

decode Method:

Converts a list of token IDs back to text by mapping each ID to its corresponding token.

Joins tokens into a string and removes excess spaces around punctuation for a natural result.

The implementation successfully encodes text by mapping each token to an integer ID based on a predefined vocabulary. The decode method converts the IDs back into readable text, maintaining punctuation and structure. However, when new text with words not in the vocabulary is used (e.g., "Hello" in "Hello, do you like tea?"), a KeyError is raised, illustrating the importance of a comprehensive vocabulary. To handle unknown tokens, we could add special tokens, like [UNK] for unknown words or [PAD] for padding sequences, providing a way to handle out-of-vocabulary tokens gracefully. This improvement is essential in real-world LLMs, which require robust handling of diverse and dynamic text inputs.

2.4 Adding Context-Specific Tokens

Byte Pair Encoding (BPE) is a sophisticated tokenisation scheme used in many Large Language Model s (LLMs) such as GPT-2, GPT-3, and ChatGPT. BPE allows for handling both known and unknown words by breaking down unfamiliar words into smaller subword units, such as common character combinations. This ensures that, even if a word was not seen in training, it can still be represented through its subcomponents, making BPE robust and flexible for handling diverse text.

To implement BPE efficiently, we can use the open-source tiktoken library developed by OpenAI. This library, implemented in Rust for speed, provides a simple interface for BPE-based tokenization. Let's walk through the steps of setting up and using the tiktoken library.

Installing and Setting Up tiktoken

To install the tiktoken library, open a terminal and run:

```
pip install tiktoken
```

After installation, you can check the version to ensure compatibility.

```
# Importing necessary libraries

from importlib.metadata import version

import tiktoken

# Print the installed version of tiktoken

print("tiktoken version:", version("tiktoken"))
```

Using the BPE Tokenizer in tiktoken

Once installed, you can instantiate the BPE tokenizer and use it to encode and decode text. Here's how to do it.

```
# Instantiate the BPE tokenizer for GPT-2
tokenizer = tiktoken.get_encoding("gpt2")
# Sample text for tokenization
text = (
    "Hello, do you like tea? <|endoftext|> In the sunlit terraces"
    " of someunknownPlace."
)
# Encode the text into token IDs, specifying allowed special tokens
integers = tokenizer.encode(text, allowed_special={"<|endoftext|>"})
```

```
# Print the encoded token IDs
print("Encoded Token IDs:", integers)
```

Explanation of Code:

Instantiation: We load the BPE tokeniser designed for GPT-2, which is also used for many GPT-like models.

Encoding: The encode method converts the input text into a list of token IDs. The allowed_special parameter specifies tokens (like <|endoftext|>) that should be preserved.

Output: The tokeniser returns a list of token IDs that correspond to words, subwords, and special characters in the text.

Expected Output:

Encoded Token IDs: [15496, 11, 466, 345, 588, 8887, 30, 220, 50256, 554, 262, 4252, 18250, 8812, 2114, 286, 617, 34680, 27271, 13]
Decoding Token IDs Back to Text
Using the decode method, we can convert the list of token IDs back into readable text, similar to how we would reverse the encoding process.

```
# Decode the token IDs back into text
decoded_text = tokenizer.decode(integers)

# Print the decoded text
print("Decoded Text:", decoded_text)
```

Expected Output:

Decoded Text: Hello, do you like tea? <|endoftext|> In the sunlit terraces of someunknownPlace.

Key Observations with BPE Tokenization

Special Tokens: The <|endoftext|> token is assigned a high token ID (50256), which is characteristic of GPT-2's vocabulary containing 50,257 tokens. This high ID allows it to be easily identified and used as a delimiter in the model's processing.

Handling Unknown Words: BPE tokenizes words that aren't in its predefined vocabulary, such as some unknown place, by breaking them down into smaller subword units or characters. This flexible breakdown allows the tokeniser to process any text input, regardless of whether each word is in its training vocabulary.

The BPE algorithm builds its vocabulary by merging frequent character pairs iteratively:

- It starts by adding individual characters as tokens.
- Then, it merges character pairs that frequently appear together into subwords.

For example, in English, "d" and "e" might merge to form "de," a common unit found in words like "define," "depend," or "hidden."

This iterative process continues until a vocabulary of a target size is reached, allowing BPE to represent words as combinations of subword units based on the most frequent patterns. The BPE tokeniser provided by tiktoken offers a powerful way to handle known and unknown words without requiring a special <|unk|> token. This flexibility, achieved by breaking down words into subword tokens, is essential for building robust LLMs that can process diverse and complex language inputs. The tiktoken library makes this process efficient and accessible, providing an easy-to-use tool for tokenising text in modern LLMs.

2.5 Implementing Byte Pair Encoding

Byte Pair Encoding (BPE) is an advanced tokenization method used in many Large Language Model s (LLMs) like GPT-2, GPT-3, and the original ChatGPT model. BPE is particularly powerful because it can effectively handle both known and unknown words by breaking down unfamiliar words into smaller, meaningful subword units or character sequences. This ability makes BPE a robust option for diverse and complex text processing.

To simplify the implementation of BPE, we can use the open-source tiktoken library by OpenAI, which is written in Rust for efficiency. This library provides a highly optimised BPE tokenizer.

Installation and Setup:

To install tiktoken, open a terminal and use Python's pip installer:

```
pip install tiktoken
```

After installation, you can check the version to confirm compatibility:

```
from importlib.metadata import version
import tiktoken
print("tiktoken version:", version("tiktoken"))
```

Using the BPE Tokenizer:

Once tiktoken is installed, we can instantiate a BPE tokenizer. Here's how to initialise and use it to encode and decode text:

```
# Initialize the BPE tokenizer for the GPT-2 model
```

```
tokenizer = tiktoken.get_encoding("gpt2")

# Sample text to tokenize
text = (
    "Hello, do you like tea? <|endoftext|> In the sunlit terraces"
    " of someunknownPlace."
)

# Encode the text into token IDs, allowing the special token <|endoftext|>
integers = tokenizer.encode(text, allowed_special={"<|endoftext|>"})

# Display the encoded token IDs
print("Encoded Token IDs:", integers)
```

Encoded Token IDs: [15496, 11, 466, 345, 588, 8887, 30, 220, 50256, 554, 262, 4252, 18250, 8812, 2114, 286, 617, 34680, 27271, 13]

Decoding Token IDs to Text:

The BPE tokenizer also allows us to reverse the process, converting token IDs back into readable text:

```
# Decode the token IDs back into text
decoded_text = tokenizer.decode(integers)

# Display the decoded text
print("Decoded Text:", decoded_text)
```

Decoded Text: Hello, do you like tea? <|endoftext|> In the sunlit terraces of someunknownPlace.

Explanation:

Tokenizer Initialization: The BPE tokenizer is set up for the GPT-2 model's vocabulary, which is compatible with many LLMs.

Encoding: The encode method converts the text into a sequence of token IDs. We use allowed_special to keep the <|endoftext|> token intact.

Output: The output is a list of token IDs representing words, subwords, and special tokens in the text.

Two important insights emerge from observing the token IDs and decoded text in a Byte Pair Encoding (BPE) tokenizer, widely used in models like GPT-2, GPT-3, and the original ChatGPT.

Special Token IDs: The <|endoftext|> token, which marks the end of text in these models, is assigned a high token ID, specifically 50,256. This ID assignment is significant because it reflects the structure of GPT's BPE vocabulary, which has a total of 50,257 unique tokens. The high token ID of <|endoftext|> ensures that this special marker stands out, allowing the model to handle text boundaries consistently and effectively during processing.

Handling Unknown Words Without <|unk|> Tokens: One of BPE's strengths is its ability to tokenize words that are not in the predefined vocabulary without needing a generic <|unk|> (unknown) token. This is achieved by breaking down unfamiliar or complex words into smaller subword units or, if necessary, individual characters. For instance, a novel word like some unknown place is tokenized into smaller, familiar units such as common prefixes, suffixes, or frequently occurring character pairs. These smaller subword tokens are already present in the vocabulary due to BPE's iterative merging process.

This flexibility is key to BPE's robustness: if the tokenizer encounters a previously unseen or rare word, it doesn't discard it as unknown but instead reconstructs it from smaller, known parts. This capability allows language models trained with BPE to handle diverse, unexpected inputs seamlessly, making it especially useful in real-world applications where input can vary significantly from training data.

How BPE Achieves Flexibility Through Subword Tokenization?

The BPE algorithm begins with a vocabulary of individual characters. It then iteratively combines frequent character pairs to form subword units, based on their frequency in the training data. For example, if "d" and "e" frequently appear together, they may be merged into "de," forming a subword that can be used across various words like "depend," "define," and "made." By building up from character-level tokens to larger subword units, BPE captures common language patterns while maintaining flexibility. This merging process continues until a target vocabulary size is reached.

As a result, BPE can decompose any new word into a sequence of tokens that, while not necessarily part of the original vocabulary as a whole word, are still meaningful at the subword level. This decomposition ensures that Large Language Model s like GPT-2 and GPT-3 can process and understand words and phrases that are new, complex, or specific to certain contexts—without needing additional unknown tokens.

The ability to break down unfamiliar words into individual characters or smaller subword units allows the tokenizer—and ultimately the Large Language Model (LLM) trained with it—to process any text, even if it contains words that were not present in its training data. This flexibility is especially valuable when handling specialized terminology, rare names, or newly coined words.

While a detailed explanation of Byte Pair Encoding (BPE) is beyond this scope, the core concept involves building a vocabulary by iteratively merging frequently occurring characters into subwords, and then merging these subwords into larger word units. BPE initially starts with each individual character as a separate token in the vocabulary (such as "a," "b," and "c"). Next, it identifies character combinations that frequently appear together and merges them to create subwords.

For example, the characters "c" and "o" might merge to form "co," which is common in words like "connect," "cooperate," and "companion." Over time, larger combinations might be merged, such as "co" and "mp" to form "comp," frequently found in words like "computer," "company," and "compare." These merges are chosen based on a frequency threshold in the dataset, ensuring that common patterns are captured.

This merging process allows the BPE tokenizer to efficiently represent new and complex words through familiar subword components, which the model has already learned during training. As a result, the LLM can handle a vast range of language inputs by representing any word, no matter how rare or specific, as a sequence of known tokens.

2.6 Sampling Data with a Sliding Window Technique

The next phase in preparing embeddings for a Large Language Model (LLM) involves creating input–target pairs, which are essential for training. But what exactly are these input–target pairs? In Pretraining, LLMs are typically trained using a next-word prediction task. This means the model is fed a sequence of words (the input) and is tasked with predicting the word that logically follows in the sequence (the target). By repeatedly learning to predict the next word, the model gradually develops an understanding of grammar, syntax, and context, enabling it to generate coherent text on its own.

For instance, given the input sequence "the man is walking" the model's target is to predict the next word, such as "down" or "slowly." Once the model successfully predicts the next word, the training window shifts forward by one word, using "the man is walking down" as the new input and aiming to predict the subsequent word based on the updated sequence.

This approach, known as Causal Language Modeling, is fundamental to training transformer-based models like GPT. By continually learning to predict each next word, the model captures a nuanced understanding of both short-term and long-term dependencies within the text, allowing it to handle complex sentences, varied topics, and diverse styles. This input-target pairing strategy enables LLMs to generate natural, contextually relevant responses based on the input they receive during inference or usage.

To train a Large Language Model (LLM) effectively, we need a data loader that generates input–target pairs for the next-word prediction task. Using a sliding window approach, this data loader will extract sequences from the training dataset where each sequence serves as an input, and the model's task is to predict the next word in the sequence.

Here, we'll use Byte Pair Encoding (BPE) to tokenize Edith Wharton's short story The Verdict. We'll then create input–target pairs, where the inputs represent a series of tokens, and the targets are the corresponding tokens shifted by one position.

Step 1: Tokenizing the Text Using BPE

First, we load and tokenize the text file using the BPE tokenizer. This step converts the entire text into a sequence of token IDs.

```
# Open the text file and read the content
with open("the-verdict.txt", "r", encoding="utf-8") as f:
    raw_text = f.read()
# Encode the text using the BPE tokenizer
enc_text = tokenizer.encode(raw_text)
# Print the total number of tokens in the dataset
print("Total tokens:", len(enc_text))
```

Expected output: 5145 (or similar)

Step 2: Creating a Sample Subset for Demonstration

To make the example more manageable, we'll remove the first 50 tokens from the dataset. This subset will provide a more varied text sample for creating input–target pairs.

```
# Create a sample subset by removing the first 50 tokens
enc_sample = enc_text[50:]
```

Step 3: Creating Input–Target Pairs for Next-Word Prediction

One simple method to create input–target pairs is to use two variables, x (input tokens) and y (target tokens). The target tokens are the input tokens shifted by one position.

```
# Define the context size for the input tokens
context_size = 4  # Number of tokens in each input sequence

# Create the input tokens (x) and target tokens (y)
x = enc_sample[:context_size]
y = enc_sample[1:context_size + 1]

# Print the input and target tokens
```

```
print(f"x: {x}")
print(f"y: {y}")
```

Expected Output:

x: [290, 4920, 2241, 287]
y: [4920, 2241, 287, 257]

Step 4: Sliding Window Approach for Sequential Input–Target Pairs

Using a sliding window approach, we can generate input–target pairs iteratively, moving one token at a time to produce each new sequence. Here, we also print the decoded text to see the input and target words in a human-readable format.

```
# Generate input–target pairs with a sliding window approach
for i in range(1, context_size + 1):
    context = enc_sample[:i]  # Input tokens
    desired = enc_sample[i]   # Target token
    print(tokenizer.decode(context), "---->", tokenizer.decode([desired]))
```

Expected Output (in text format):

```
and ----> established
and established ----> himself
and established himself ----> in
and established himself in ----> a
```

The following code defines a GPT DatasetV1 class, a dataset class based on PyTorch's Dataset that efficiently generates batched input–target pairs. Each row in the dataset contains a sequence of token IDs as the input and the next sequence of token IDs as the target, both of which are generated using a sliding window approach with a specified maximum length and stride.

Code Implementation

```
import torch

from torch.utils.data import Dataset, DataLoader

class GPTDatasetV1(Dataset):
    def __init__(self, txt, tokenizer, max_length, stride):
        """

        Initializes the dataset by generating input and target sequences.

        :param txt: Raw text to be tokenized
        :param tokenizer: Tokenizer to convert text to token IDs
```

```
        :param max_length: Maximum length of each input sequence
        :param stride: Step size between each sequence start
        """
        self.input_ids = []
        self.target_ids = []

        # Tokenize the entire text to get token IDs
        token_ids = tokenizer.encode(txt)

        # Create input-target pairs with a sliding window approach
        for i in range(0, len(token_ids) - max_length, stride):
            # Input sequence of length `max_length`
            input_chunk = token_ids[i:i + max_length]
            # Target sequence is shifted by one position
            target_chunk = token_ids[i + 1: i + max_length + 1]

            # Store the input and target sequences as tensors
            self.input_ids.append(torch.tensor(input_chunk))
            self.target_ids.append(torch.tensor(target_chunk))
    def __len__(self):
        """
        Returns the total number of samples in the dataset.
        """
        return len(self.input_ids)

    def __getitem__(self, idx):
        """
        Fetches the input and target sequence tensors for a given index.

        :param idx: Index of the sample to retrieve
        :return: Tuple of (Input Tensor, Target Tensor)
        """
        return self.input_ids[idx], self.target_ids[idx]
```

Explanation of Code

Initialization (__init__ method):

- *txt:* The raw text data to be tokenized.
- *tokenizer:* A tokenizer that converts the text into a sequence of token IDs.
- *max_length:* Defines the length of each input sequence (input chunk).

- *stride:* Specifies the step size to move along the text when creating each new input–target pair.
- The input_chunk represents a sequence of tokens, and the target_chunk is the same sequence shifted by one position. This way, each token in target_chunk is the expected "next word" for the corresponding position in input_chunk.

  __len__ Method:

- Returns the number of input–target pairs generated, based on the total tokenized text length, max_length, and stride.

  __getitem__ Method:

- Fetches a sample at the specified index, returning the input and target sequences as tensors.

Using the Dataset with a DataLoader

Combining GPT DatasetV1 with PyTorch's DataLoader will allow us to iterate over batches of input–target pairs for efficient training.

```
# Initialize the dataset with sample text and tokenizer

dataset = GPTDatasetV1(txt=raw_text, tokenizer=tokenizer, max_length=50, stride=5)

# Create a DataLoader to generate batches of data

data_loader = DataLoader(dataset, batch_size=2, shuffle=True)

# Test the DataLoader by iterating over a batch

for batch_input, batch_target in data_loader:
    print("Batch Input: ", batch_input)
    print("Batch Target: ", batch_target)
    break  # Display only the first batch for demonstration
```

Using GPT DatasetV1 with a Data Loader enables efficient batch processing, where each batch consists of paired input and target sequences. This approach prepares the dataset for training, allowing the model to learn next-word predictions over consecutive tokens within each sequence.

The following code defines a create_dataloader_v1 function, which builds a PyTorch data loader using the GPTDatasetV1 dataset. This setup generates batches of input–target pairs for Large Language Model (LLM) training, using a sliding window approach to shift the input across batches. This method provides a flexible way to control batch size, context length, and the degree of overlap between consecutive input sequences via the stride parameter.

Data Loader Implementation:

```
import torch

from torch.utils.data import Dataset, DataLoader

def create_dataloader_v1(txt, batch_size=4, max_length=256, stride=128, shuffle=True, drop_last=True, num_workers=0):

    “””

    Creates a data loader that generates batches of input–target pairs for training.

    :param txt: The raw text data to be tokenized

    :param batch_size: Number of input–target pairs in each batch

    :param max_length: Length of each input sequence

    :param stride: Step size for moving the window across the text

    :param shuffle: Whether to shuffle the dataset

    :param drop_last: Whether to drop the last batch if it is incomplete

    :param num_workers: Number of worker threads for data loading

    :return: A PyTorch DataLoader object

    “””

    # Initialize tokenizer and dataset

    tokenizer = tiktoken.get_encoding(“gpt2”)

    dataset = GPTDatasetV1(txt, tokenizer, max_length, stride)

    # Create a DataLoader for batching data

    dataloader = DataLoader(

        dataset,

batch_size=batch_size,
```

```
        shuffle=shuffle,
        drop_last=drop_last,
        num_workers=num_workers
    )
    return dataloader
```

Testing the Data Loader with a Small Batch Size:

We can now test this data loader with a batch size of 1 and a small context size of 4. This setup will help illustrate how GPT DatasetV1 and create_dataloader_v1 work together to generate sequential input–target pairs for next-word prediction.

```
# Load the text file
with open("the-verdict.txt", "r", encoding="utf-8") as f:
    raw_text = f.read()
# Create the data loader with batch size 1, max_length 4, and stride 1
dataloader = create_dataloader_v1(raw_text, batch_size=1, max_length=4, stride=1, shuffle=False)
# Initialize an iterator to fetch data from the data loader
data_iter = iter(dataloader)
first_batch = next(data_iter)
# Print the first batch of input and Target Tensors
print(first_batch)
```

Expected Output:

[tensor([[40, 367, 2885, 1464]]), tensor([[367, 2885, 1464, 1807]])]

Explanation:

The first batch contains two tensors: the Input Tensor and the Target Tensor. Since max_length is set to 4, each tensor contains four token IDs. Here, the Input Tensor represents a sequence of tokens, and the Target Tensor is shifted by one position, which means each element in the Target Tensor is the next token following the corresponding element in the Input Tensor.

Exploring the Effect of stride=1

To understand how the stride=1 parameter affects the data loader, we can fetch another batch from the data iterator.

Fetch the next batch from the data loader

second_batch = next(data_iter)

print(second_batch)

Expected Output:

[tensor([[367, 2885, 1464, 1807]]), tensor([[2885, 1464, 1807, 3619]])]

Explanation:

The input sequence in the second batch is shifted by one token compared to the first batch.This sliding window approach, controlled by stride, enables consecutive batches to share overlapping sequences, helping the model learn context across shifts.

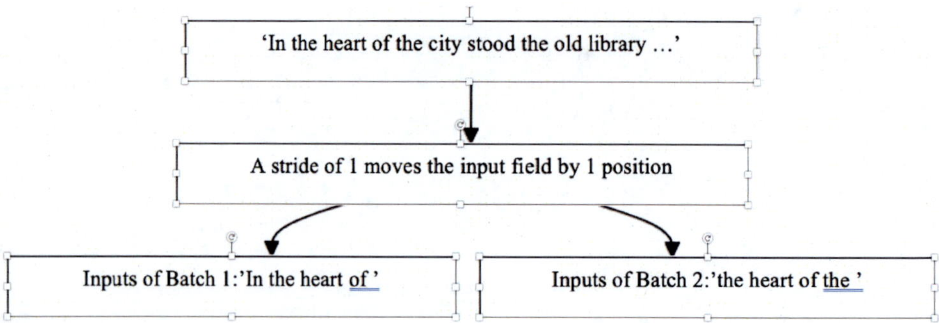

Testing the Data Loader with a Larger Batch Size

To observe the data loader's behavior with a larger batch size and a non-overlapping stride, we set batch_size=8 and stride=4. This configuration allows each batch to contain unique token sequences without overlap, reducing the risk of overfitting.

Create the data loader with batch size 8, max_length 4, and stride 4

dataloader = create_dataloader_v1(raw_text, batch_size=8, max_length=4, stride=4, shuffle=False)

Initialize an iterator to fetch data from the data loader

data_iter = iter(dataloader)

```
inputs, targets = next(data_iter)

# Print the batched inputs and targets

print("Inputs:\n", inputs)

print("\nTargets:\n", targets)
```

Expected Output:

Inputs:

```
tensor([[   40,   367,  2885,  1464],
        [ 1807,  3619,   402,   271],
        [10899,  2138,   257,  7026],
        [15632,   438,  2016,   257],
        [  922,  5891,  1576,   438],
        [  568,   340,   373,   645],
        [ 1049,  5975,   284,   502],
        [  284,  3285,   326,    11]])
```

Targets:

```
tensor([[  367,  2885,  1464,  1807],
        [ 3619,   402,   271, 10899],
        [ 2138,   257,  7026, 15632],
        [  438,  2016,   257,   922],
        [ 5891,  1576,   438,   568],
        [  340,   373,   645,  1049],
        [ 5975,   284,   502,   284],
        [ 3285,   326,    11,   287]])
```

Explanation:

- The stride=4 setting ensures non-overlapping batches, meaning each input–target pair in the batch represents a unique sequence without shared tokens between consecutive batches.
- Larger batch sizes allow the model to learn from more data simultaneously, but may require more memory. This is a typical tradeoff in deep learning: smaller

batches use less memory and can generalise better in some cases, while larger batches provide stability and faster training.

This create_dataloader_v1 function with GPT DatasetV1 allows for flexible batching, with control over input length, stride, and overlap, making it suitable for efficiently training LLMs on next-word prediction tasks.

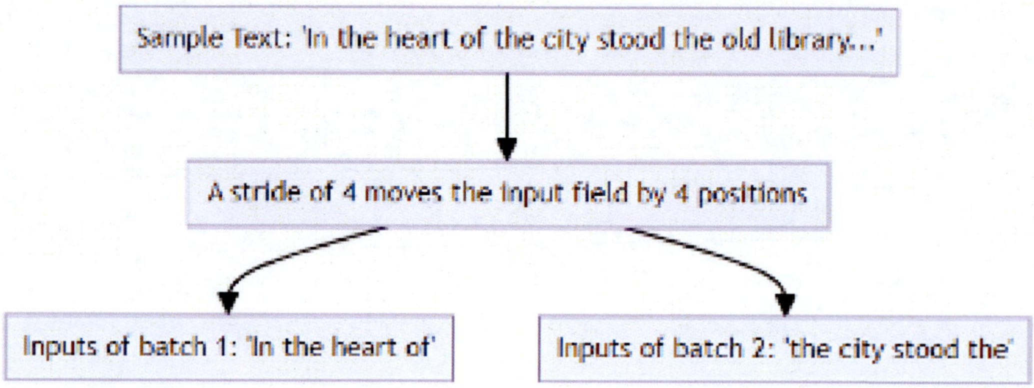

2.7 Creating Embeddings for Tokens

The final step in preparing input text for training Large Language Models (LLMs) involves converting token IDs into embedding vectors. These embedding vectors represent words or tokens in a continuous numerical space, which is essential for deep neural networks. Neural networks like GPT use backpropagation to optimize these embeddings during training.

Token IDs alone are categorical and not suitable for the numerical computations required in neural networks. Embeddings transform these IDs into dense, continuous-valued vectors that capture the semantic and syntactic properties of words. For efficiency, embedding layers in frameworks like PyTorch allow direct mapping from token IDs to embeddings using a pre-initialized weight matrix.

Hands-On Example: Embedding Layer in PyTorch

Step 1: Define Input Tokens and Vocabulary

We start by defining the input tokens and vocabulary size. For simplicity:

Assume the vocabulary size is 6 (instead of tens of thousands in actual models like GPT). Use an embedding size of 3 to represent each token in three dimensions.

```
import torch

# Define token IDs for input

input_ids = torch.tensor([2, 3, 5, 1])

# Define vocabulary size and embedding dimensions

vocab_size = 6  # Number of unique tokens

output_dim = 3  # Embedding dimensions
```

Step 2: Initialize the Embedding Layer

The embedding layer is initialised with random values that will be optimised during training. We set a random seed for reproducibility.

```
# Set random seed for reproducibility

torch.manual_seed(123)

# Initialize the embedding layer

embedding_layer = torch.nn.Embedding(vocab_size, output_dim)

# Print the weight matrix of the embedding layer

print("Embedding Layer Weights:\n", embedding_layer.weight)
```

Output: The embedding layer's weight matrix contains random values with dimensions [vocab_size × output_dim]. Each row corresponds to a token, and each column represents an embedding dimension.

```
tensor([[ 0.3374, -0.1778, -0.1690],
        [ 0.9178,  1.5810,  1.3010],
        [ 1.2753, -0.2010, -0.1606],
        [-0.4015,  0.9666, -1.1481],
        [-1.1589,  0.3255, -0.6315],
        [-2.8400, -0.7849, -1.4096]], requires_grad=True)
```

Step 3: Retrieve Embedding Vectors for Token IDs

The embedding layer acts as a lookup table. Each token ID maps to its corresponding row in the weight matrix.

```
# Retrieve the embedding vector for a single token ID
```

```
single_embedding = embedding_layer(torch.tensor([3]))

print("Embedding for Token ID 3:\n", single_embedding)
```

Output: The embedding for token ID 3 corresponds to the fourth row of the weight matrix:

```
tensor([[-0.4015,  0.9666, -1.1481]], grad_fn=<EmbeddingBackward0>)
```

Step 4: Convert Multiple Token IDs to Embedding Vectors

The embedding layer can process multiple token IDs at once, returning a matrix where each row corresponds to an embedding vector for a token.

```
# Retrieve embeddings for multiple token IDs
all_embeddings = embedding_layer(input_ids)
print("Embeddings for All Token IDs:\n", all_embeddings)
```

Output: The result is a 4 × 3 matrix, where each row represents the embedding vector for a corresponding token ID.

```
tensor([[ 1.2753, -0.2010, -0.1606],
        [-0.4015,  0.9666, -1.1481],
        [-2.8400, -0.7849, -1.4096],
        [ 0.9178,  1.5810,  1.3010]], grad_fn=<EmbeddingBackward0>)
```

Embedding Weight Matrix: The embedding layer uses a weight matrix with dimensions [vocab_size × output_dim].Each token ID corresponds to a row in this matrix.

Lookup Operation: Instead of using computationally expensive one-hot encoding followed by matrix multiplication, embedding layers efficiently perform direct lookups.

Optimization During Training: The embedding weights are initialized randomly but are optimised during training via back propagation, allowing the model to learn meaningful representations of words or tokens.

Comparison to One-Hot Encoding: Using one-hot encoding involves creating sparse vectors for tokens and multiplying them by a weight matrix, which is computationally inefficient. Embedding layers simplify this process while achieving the same result.

Embedding layers provide a dense representation of words but lack information about the position of tokens in a sequence. The next step in preparing input data involves encoding this positional information, enabling the model to understand the order and relationships between tokens in a sequence. This is critical for tasks requiring context comprehension, such as next-word prediction.

2.8 Position Encoding for Words

Token embeddings provide a rich numerical representation of text data, but they lack any information about the order of tokens in a sequence. Since the self-attention mechanism in transformer-based models like GPT is inherently position-agnostic, the model cannot distinguish between sequences like "The cat chased the dog" and "The dog chased the cat" without additional position-aware information. To address this, positional embeddings are added to token embeddings, encoding the position of each token within a sequence.

Types of Positional Embeddings

- Absolute Positional Embeddings: Assign a unique vector to each position in the sequence. These embeddings explicitly encode the exact position of each token.
- Relative Positional Embeddings: Capture the relationship between tokens based on their distance. These embeddings focus on how far apart tokens are rather than their absolute positions.

OpenAI's GPT models use absolute positional embeddings, where a learnable positional embedding is added to each token embedding. These embeddings are optimised during model training, ensuring they adapt to the data and task.

Step-by-Step Implementation of Positional Embeddings

Step 1: Define Vocabulary and Embedding Dimensions

We begin by defining the vocabulary size and embedding dimensions. For this demonstration:

- **Vocabulary Size:** 50,257 (typical of GPT models trained with Byte Pair Encoding).
- **Embedding Dimensions:** 256 (smaller than GPT-3's 12,288 dimensions but sufficient for experimentation).

```
import torch
# Define vocabulary size and embedding dimensions
vocab_size = 50257  # Typical GPT vocabulary size
output_dim = 256    # Embedding dimension size
```

Step 2: Initialize Token Embedding Layer

The token embedding layer maps token IDs to 256-dimensional vectors.

```
# Initialize token embedding layer
```

token_embedding_layer = torch.nn.Embedding(vocab_size, output_dim)

Step 3: Generate Sample Token IDs

We create a batch of token IDs using a data loader. For simplicity:

- **Batch Size:** 8
- **Tokens Per Sample:** 4

```
# Simulated data loader output: batch of token IDs

inputs = torch.tensor([
    [40, 367, 2885, 1464],
    [1807, 3619, 402, 271],
    [10899, 2138, 257, 7026],
    [15632, 438, 2016, 257],
    [922, 5891, 1576, 438],
    [568, 340, 373, 645],
    [1049, 5975, 284, 502],
    [284, 3285, 326, 11]
])

print("Token IDs:\n", inputs)

print("\nInput Shape:\n", inputs.shape)
```

Output:

```
Token IDs:
tensor([[   40,   367,  2885,  1464],
        [ 1807,  3619,   402,   271],
        [10899,  2138,   257,  7026],
        [15632,   438,  2016,   257],
        [  922,  5891,  1576,   438],
        [  568,   340,   373,   645],
        [ 1049,  5975,   284,   502],
        [  284,  3285,   326,    11]])
```

Input Shape:

```
torch.Size([8, 4])
```

Step 4: Convert Token IDs to Embeddings

The embedding layer converts the 8 × 4 token ID matrix into an 8 × 4 × 256 tensor.

```
# Convert token IDs to embeddings

token_embeddings = token_embedding_layer(inputs)

print("Token Embeddings Shape:\n", token_embeddings.shape)
```

Output:

Token Embeddings Shape:

torch.Size([8, 4, 256])

Each of the 32 tokens (8 samples × 4 tokens per sample) is now represented as a 256-dimensional vector.

Step 5: Create Positional Embedding Layer

We create a positional embedding layer with the same embedding dimension as the token embedding layer. This layer assigns a unique vector to each position in a sequence.

```
# Define context length (maximum tokens per input)

context_length = inputs.shape[1]

# Initialize positional embedding layer

pos_embedding_layer = torch.nn.Embedding(context_length, output_dim)

# Generate positional embeddings for each position (0, 1, ..., context_length-1)

pos_embeddings = pos_embedding_layer(torch.arange(context_length))

print("Positional Embeddings Shape:\n", pos_embeddings.shape)
```

Output:

Positional Embeddings Shape:
torch.Size([4, 256])

Step 6: Add Token and Positional Embeddings

The positional embeddings are added to the token embeddings, resulting in position-aware token representations.

```
# Add positional embeddings to token embeddings
```

```
input_embeddings = token_embeddings + pos_embeddings
print("Input Embeddings Shape:\n", input_embeddings.shape)
```

Output:

```
Input Embeddings Shape:
 torch.Size([8, 4, 256])
```

- **Position-Aware Representations:** Adding positional embeddings to token embeddings allows the model to capture the sequential order of tokens.
- **Learnable Embeddings:** Both token and positional embeddings are initialized randomly and optimized during training, enabling the model to adapt to specific tasks and datasets.
- **Efficient Implementation:** PyTorch's embedding layers provide an efficient way to handle both token and positional embeddings, avoiding the need for explicit one-hot encodings.
- **Scalability:** This approach scales well for larger vocabulary sizes and embedding dimensions, making it suitable for large-scale LLMs like GPT-4.

By combining token embeddings with positional embeddings, we have created input representations that include both the content and position of each token. This position-aware input embedding is essential for transformer-based models to generate context-aware and coherent predictions. These embeddings form the foundation for further processing by the LLM, which we will explore in subsequent chapters.

SUMMARY

- ✓ The chapter explains the need to convert raw text into continuous vector representations (embeddings) to enable neural networks to process numerical data.
- ✓ Tokenization is discussed as the process of dividing text into smaller units (words, subwords, or characters) for easier processing, with methods like Byte Pair Encoding (BPE) highlighted for handling diverse vocabularies.
- ✓ Token IDs are generated from tokens using a predefined vocabulary, which maps each unique token to an integer, forming the basis for numerical processing.
- ✓ Embedding layers in PyTorch are used to map token IDs into high-dimensional vectors, initializing these embeddings with random values that are optimized during training.

- ✓ Positional embeddings are introduced to encode the order of tokens in a sequence, addressing the self-attention mechanism's position-agnostic nature in LLMs.
- ✓ Practical examples show how to implement token and positional embeddings using PyTorch, including combining them to create position-aware input representations.
- ✓ The chapter provides insights into efficient data preparation techniques, such as sliding window data loaders, embedding optimization, and managing context lengths, laying the foundation for understanding LLM architectures.

Exercises

Exercise 1 – Multiple Choice Questions

1. Which of the following is an advantage of using embeddings in LLMs?
   a) Reduces the amount of data needed for training
   b) Converts text into a continuous vector space that neural networks can process
   c) Eliminates the need for tokenization
   d) Stores entire text data directly in raw format
2. What is the purpose of a vocabulary in tokenization?
   a) To store entire text as-is
   b) To define mappings between unique tokens and integer IDs
   c) To organize text into chapters
   d) To increase the model's size

Exercise 2 – One Word Answers

1. What type of neural network architecture is foundational to LLMs like GPT?
2. Which technique is commonly used to convert raw text into a sequence of numbers?

Exercise 3 – Short Answers

1. Why is tokenization necessary for training Large Language Models (LLMs)?
2. What is the purpose of the sliding window approach in creating input–target pairs for LLMs?

Exercise 4 – Long Answers

1. Explain how Byte-Pair Encoding (BPE) tokenizes text and why it is useful in LLMs.
2. Describe the process of creating word embeddings and their importance in LLMs.

Answers

Exercise 1- 1) b, 2) b

Exercise 2- 1) Transformer, 2) Tokenization

Online Resources

	Practice Paper	YouTube Video Playlist Link
Link	https://forms.gle/EMMrUi2RETgfwDBw7	ttps://www.youtube.com/playlist?list=PLzlh_31VWEFq78f32uTDuWxcVpT088H6L
QR Code		

Chapter 3

DEVELOPING ATTENTION MECHANISMS

In this chapter you will learn about:

- ☐ Addressing Challenges with Long Sequence Modeling
- ☐ Using Attention Mechanisms to Capture Dependencies
- ☐ Focusing on Different Parts of Input with
- ☐ Building Self-Attention with Trainable
- ☐ Applying Causal Attention to Mask

In this phase, we will delve into an essential component of the architecture of Large Language Model s (LLMs): attention mechanisms. These mechanisms are fundamental to how LLMs understand and generate text by focusing on different parts of the input in a dynamic and context-aware manner. Before diving into the complete LLM architecture, we will first explore attention mechanisms in detail, examining them at a conceptual and computational level to understand their inner workings.

Our discussion will focus on the process of tokenizing input text, breaking it down into individual words or subword units, and encoding these tokens into vector representations known as embeddings. These embeddings serve as the foundation for LLM computations, enabling the model to process and contextualize text effectively.

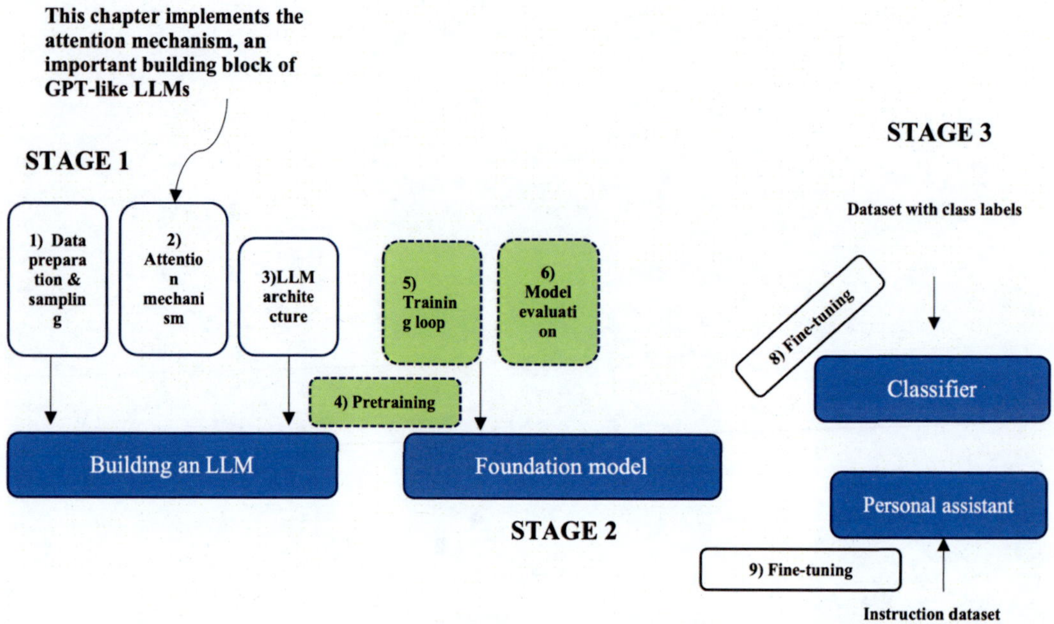

Next, we will implement and analyze four distinct variants of attention mechanisms. These variants represent an evolutionary progression of the attention concept, with each iteration introducing improvements in efficiency, scalability, and adaptability. The ultimate goal of this exploration is to develop a robust and compact implementation of multi-head attention, a cornerstone of modern LLMs.

Multi-head attention facilitates the model's ability to attend to different parts of the input simultaneously, capturing diverse relationships and patterns within the data. By experimenting with these attention variants, we will not only gain a deeper understanding of their mechanics, but also prepare to integrate them seamlessly into a larger LLM framework.

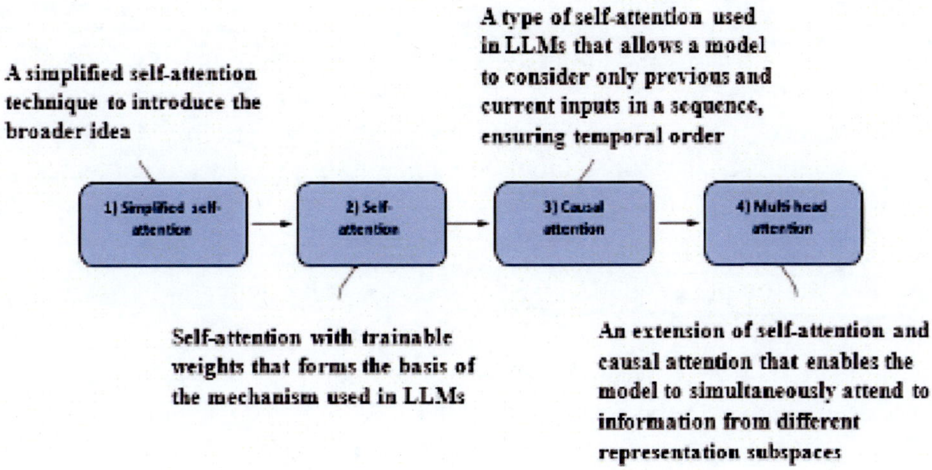

After mastering the standalone attention mechanisms, we will move on to implement the other essential components of an LLM, combining them with self-attention to build a complete model capable of generating text. This process will allow us to observe the practical application and performance of attention mechanisms within the broader context of LLMs, paving the way for further innovations and optimisations in subsequent chapters.

3.1 Addressing Challenges with Long Sequence Modeling

Before delving into the intricacies of self-attention mechanisms, which lie at the core of modern Large Language Models (LLMs), it's helpful to understand the limitations of pre-LLM architectures that did not incorporate attention mechanisms. A simple word-by-word translation approach often fails because different languages have unique grammatical structures and syntax. This complexity requires a more nuanced understanding of the entire sentence or context. To address these challenges, deep neural networks were traditionally structured with two key components: an Encoder and a Decoder. The Encoder's role is to read and process the input text to generate a representation of its meaning, while the Decoder generates the translated output based on this representation. This architecture is foundational to sequence-to-sequence (Seq2Seq) models.

Early Encoder-Decoder Models with RNNs

Before the advent of transformers, Recurrent Neural Networks (RNNs) were the backbone of Encoder-Decoder models for tasks like language translation. RNNs are designed to process sequential data by taking the output of one step as input to the next step, making them suitable for handling text data, where order matters. In an Encoder-Decoder setup using RNNs:

1. The Encoder processes the input sequence one token at a time. At each step, it updates its internal "hidden state," which is meant to capture the context of the input sequence up to that point. By the time the Encoder finishes processing the input, it condenses the entire input sequence into a single hidden state, often referred to as a "context vector" or an embedding.
2. The Decoder then starts with this final hidden state from the Encoder and generates the output sequence one token at a time, updating its own hidden state at each step.
3. This hidden state acts as the memory of the input sequence and guides the Decoder in producing the output.

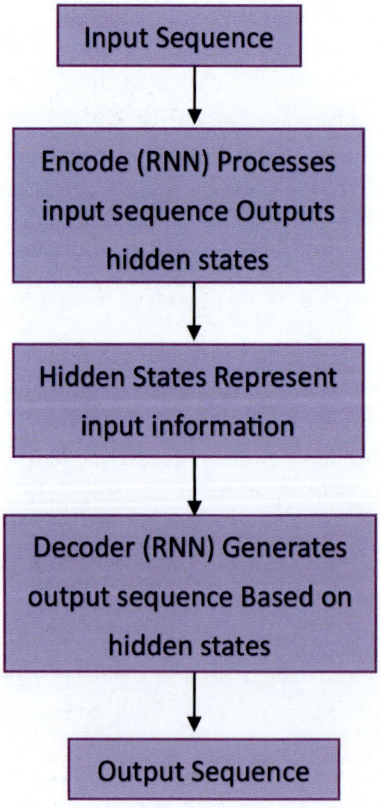

Limitations of RNN-Based Encoder-Decoder Models

While this approach was ground breaking at the time, it came with significant limitations:

- Information Bottleneck: Compressing the entire input sequence into a single hidden state can lead to a loss of important context, especially for long or complex sentences where dependencies between words span greater distances.
- Vanishing Gradient Problem: RNNs, particularly in their vanilla form, struggle to propagate gradient information over long sequences, making it difficult to retain context from earlier tokens in the sequence.
- Sequential Processing: RNNs process data step by step, which makes them inherently slow for longer sequences and prevents parallelisation during training.

As a result of these limitations, RNN-based models often failed to capture the full context required for accurate translations or other complex sequential tasks.

Enter Attention Mechanisms

The shortcomings of Encoder-Decoder RNNs paved the way for the development of attention mechanisms. Instead of relying solely on the final hidden state of the Encoder, attention mechanisms allow the Decoder to access all hidden states produced by the Encoder. This means that the Decoder can dynamically "attend" to different parts of the input sequence at each step of generating the output, enabling it to maintain context over longer distances and resolve dependencies more effectively. This innovation not only solved many of the bottlenecks associated with RNNs but also laid the foundation for the transformer architecture, which eliminates the need for RNNs altogether. Transformers leverage self-attention mechanisms to process sequences in parallel, making them both faster and more contextually aware. This paradigm shift marked the beginning of modern LLMs, enabling them to excel in tasks like translation, summarization, and text generation.

3.2 Using Attention Mechanisms to Capture Dependencies

While Recurrent Neural Networks (RNNs) work effectively for tasks involving short sequences, they struggle with longer texts. This limitation arises because RNNs do not have direct access to earlier parts of the input sequence during later steps of processing. Instead, they rely on encoding the entire input sequence into a single hidden state, which is then passed to the Decoder. This approach often results in a loss of crucial contextual information, especially when dealing with long or complex sentences.

Introduction of Attention Mechanisms

To address this challenge, researchers introduced the Bahdanau Attention Mechanism in 2014. Named after the lead author of the seminal paper, this mechanism revolutionized the Encoder-Decoder architecture by allowing the Decoder to selectively focus on different parts of the input sequence during each step of decoding. Instead of compressing all the information into a single hidden state, Bahdanau attention enables the Decoder to dynamically access the relevant hidden states from the Encoder. This significantly improved the model's ability to handle long-range dependencies and context.

The Evolution Towards Transformers

Just three years later, in 2017, researchers proposed the Transformer Architecture, which marked a paradigm shift in Natural Language Processing (NLP). This architecture demonstrated that RNNs were not necessary for building powerful sequence models. Instead, the transformer introduced a novel mechanism known as self-attention, which was inspired by the principles of Bahdanau attention but extended to operate on an entirely new level.

Self-attention allows each position in an input sequence to evaluate the relevance of all other positions in the sequence when generating its representation. Unlike the sequential processing of RNNs, self-attention processes the input in parallel, enabling it to capture relationships between words across the entire sequence efficiently. This parallelism makes transformers not only faster, but also more effective at capturing global context.

Self-Attention in Modern Language Models

Self-attention has since become the cornerstone of contemporary LLMs, including popular models like the GPT series. It enables these models to understand and generate text by focusing on different parts of the input sequence dynamically, ensuring that critical contextual relationships are maintained.

We will explore the coding and implementation of self-attention mechanisms, with a focus on their role within transformer-based architectures like GPT. We will break down how self-attention computes relationships between tokens in an input sequence and integrate this information into embeddings. This understanding will set the stage for building the remaining components of LLMs in the next chapter. By mastering self-attention, you will gain a deeper appreciation for how modern LLMs achieve their remarkable performance in understanding and generating human language. This mechanism is not just a key innovation in AI but also the foundation for the advanced capabilities of today's NLP systems.

3.3 Focusing on Different Parts of Input with Self-Attention

The self-attention mechanism forms the backbone of modern transformer-based architectures, such as GPT models. It enables models to compute relationships between different parts of an input sequence, providing enriched context to enhance understanding and text generation. In this step-by-step walkthrough, we will implement a simplified version of self-attention, focusing on its core functionality without trainable weights, before incorporating the complete trainable mechanism used in LLMs.

Key Concepts in Self-Attention

Self-attention computes attention weights by relating different positions within a single input sequence. Unlike traditional attention mechanisms, which focus on relationships between two sequences (e.g., an input and output sequence), self-attention dynamically assesses dependencies within the same sequence. This is crucial for tasks like text understanding and generation, where words need to be contextualised based on their relationships with other words in the same sentence or paragraph.

In this simplified implementation:

1. Input tokens are represented as embedding vectors.
2. Attention scores are computed using dot products between a query token and all tokens in the input sequence.
3. The scores are normalized using softmax to produce attention weights.
4. Context vectors are generated as a weighted sum of the input embeddings.

Input Sequence Preparation

Let's start by embedding a simple sentence into vectors.

```
import torch

# Example input embeddings for the sentence "The quick brown fox jumps over"
inputs = torch.tensor([
    [0.3, 0.1, 0.5], # The
    [0.6, 0.8, 0.7], # quick
    [0.4, 0.9, 0.2], # brown
    [0.7, 0.3, 0.6], # fox
    [0.5, 0.7, 0.8], # jumps
    [0.2, 0.4, 0.1]  # over
])

# Print the input embeddings
```

```
print("Input embeddings:\n", inputs)
```

Step 1: Compute Attention Scores

We calculate attention scores as the dot product between a query token and all tokens in the input sequence.

```
# Select a query token, e.g., the second token "quick"
query = inputs[1]  # Embedding for the token "quick"
# Initialize an empty tensor to store attention scores
attn_scores = torch.empty(inputs.shape[0])
# Compute dot product between the query and each input token
for i, x_i in enumerate(inputs):
    attn_scores[i] = torch.dot(x_i, query)
# Print the computed attention scores
print("Attention scores:\n", attn_scores)
```

Step 2: Normalize Attention Scores with Softmax

Attention scores are normalized to produce weights that sum to 1, making them interpretable as relative importance.

```
# Normalize the attention scores using softmax
attn_weights = torch.softmax(attn_scores, dim=0)
# Print the normalized attention weights
print("Attention weights:\n", attn_weights)
print("Sum of weights:", attn_weights.sum())
```

Step 3: Compute the Context Vector

The context vector is calculated as a weighted sum of the input embeddings using the attention weights.

```
# Initialize a zero tensor for the context vector
context_vec = torch.zeros(query.shape)
# Compute the weighted sum of input embeddings
for i, x_i in enumerate(inputs):
    context_vec += attn_weights[i] * x_i
```

```
# Print the computed context vector
print("Context vector:\n", context_vec)
```

1. Input Sequence Preparation: Represent tokens in the input sentence as fixed-size embedding vectors. These embeddings capture semantic information about the words.
2. Attention Score Computation: Compute the similarity between a query token and all other tokens in the sequence using the dot product. This step establishes how much "attention" each token deserves relative to the query token.
3. Normalization with Softmax: Use softmax to normalise attention scores into probabilities. This ensures that all weights are non-negative and sum to 1, maintaining numerical stability.
4. Context Vector Computation: Generate a context vector for the query token by taking a weighted sum of all input embeddings, where the weights are the normalized attention scores.

Updated Example for Numerical Stability

Instead of using a naive softmax implementation, leverage PyTorch's optimised softmax function to ensure stability and efficiency.

```
# Use PyTorch's built-in softmax for normalisation
attn_weights_stable = torch.softmax(attn_scores, dim=0)
# Print the stable attention weights
print("Stable attention weights:\n", attn_weights_stable)
print("Sum of weights (stable):", attn_weights_stable.sum())
```

Example Context Vector Interpretation

For the query token "quick," the resulting context vector is enriched with information from all other tokens in the input sequence. This enriched representation provides the necessary context for downstream tasks, such as predicting the next word in a sentence or understanding relationships between words. Once the basics of self-attention are clear, the next step is to incorporate trainable weights. This involves learning matrices for query, key, and value transformations, enabling the model to optimize the attention mechanism dynamically during training. This foundational understanding will serve as a stepping stone for building a complete multi-head self-attention mechanism, as used in state-of-the-art transformer models.

Computing Attention Weights for All Tokens: A Step-by-Step Approach

In this walkthrough, we compute the attention weights and context vectors for all tokens in an input sequence using a simplified self-attention mechanism. The goal is to enrich each token's embedding with contextual information derived from other tokens in the sequence. This process is essential for capturing relationships and dependencies within the input, forming the foundation of advanced transformer-based architectures.

We will use a matrix-based approach to improve efficiency and reduce reliance on nested loops. This method allows us to compute attention scores, normalize them, and derive context vectors for all tokens simultaneously.

Step-by-Step Code Implementation

Example Input Sequence

We begin with a sequence of tokens represented as embedding vectors. Let's consider a different example sentence: "AI models learn from data efficiently."

```
import torch

# Example input embeddings for the sentence "AI models learn from data efficiently."

inputs = torch.tensor([

    [0.5, 0.2, 0.1],  # AI

    [0.7, 0.8, 0.6],  # models

    [0.4, 0.9, 0.3],  # learn

    [0.6, 0.1, 0.8],  # from

    [0.3, 0.4, 0.2],  # data

    [0.8, 0.7, 0.5]   # efficiently

])

# Print input embeddings

print("Input embeddings:\n", inputs)
```

Step 1: Compute Attention Scores for All Tokens

Instead of computing attention scores token by token, we use matrix multiplication for efficiency.

```
# Compute attention scores using matrix multiplication
attn_scores = inputs @ inputs.T  # Dot product between all token embeddings
# Print the resulting attention score matrix
print("Attention scores:\n", attn_scores)
```

Explanation: Each element (i,j)(i, j)(i,j) in attn_scores represents the dot product between token iii and token jjj, capturing their similarity.

Step 2: Normalize Attention Scores Using Softmax

Normalize the attention scores along each row so that they sum to 1, producing interpretable attention weights.

```
# Normalize the attention scores using softmax
attn_weights = torch.softmax(attn_scores, dim=-1)
# Print the normalized attention weights
print("Attention weights:\n", attn_weights)
```

Explanation:

Softmax ensures all attention weights are positive and sum to 1 for each token. The dim=-1 parameter specifies that normalization occurs along the last dimension (i.e., rows).

Step 3: Compute Context Vectors for All Tokens

Using the attention weights, calculate context vectors for all tokens as a weighted sum of the input embeddings.

```
# Compute context vectors using matrix multiplication
context_vectors = attn_weights @ inputs  # Weighted sum of input embeddings
# Print the resulting context vectors
print("Context vectors:\n", context_vectors)
```

Explanation: Each context vector enriches a token's embedding by incorporating information from all other tokens, weighted by their relevance (attention weights).

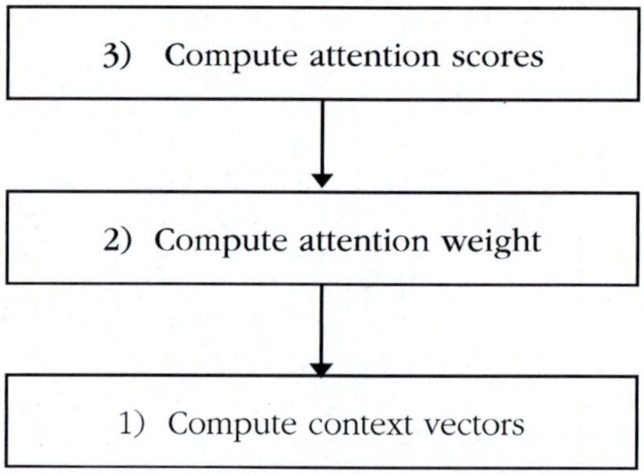

Double-Check Results

To ensure the implementation is correct, verify that the second row of the context vectors matches the previously calculated context vector for the second token (if computed manually).

```
# Example manual computation for token 2 ("models") to verify results
query = inputs[1]  # Token 2 embedding
manual_context_vec = torch.zeros(query.shape)


# Manually compute context vector for token 2
for i, x_i in enumerate(inputs):
    manual_context_vec += attn_weights[1, i] * x_i


# Compare manual and matrix-computed results
print("Manually computed context vector for token 2:\n", manual_context_vec)
print("Matrix-computed context vector for token 2:\n", context_vectors[1])
```

1. **Input Sequence Representation:** The input tokens are represented as embedding vectors, capturing their semantic meaning. Each token xix_ixi is a ddd-dimensional vector (e.g., 3D in this example).
2. **Attention Score Computation:** Dot products between token embeddings capture their pairwise similarity. The result is a square matrix, where each element indicates how strongly one token attends to another.
3. **Normalization with Softmax:** Softmax converts attention scores into probabilities (weights) that sum to 1 for each token. This step ensures interpretability and numerical stability.

4. **Context Vector Calculation:** Each token's context vector is computed as a weighted sum of all token embeddings, using the attention weights.
5. **Validation:** Verify that the computed context vectors are consistent with manual calculations for individual tokens.

The context vectors are enriched embeddings that allow tokens to "understand" their relationships with other tokens in the sequence. For example, the token "models" will have a context vector that incorporates information from related words like "AI" and "learn."

Optimized Code Version

Here is an optimized version of the full process using only matrix operations

```
import torch

# Example embeddings for a new sentence

inputs = torch.tensor([
    [0.2, 0.3, 0.4],
    [0.5, 0.6, 0.7],
    [0.1, 0.8, 0.5],
    [0.9, 0.4, 0.3]
])

# Step 1: Compute attention scores (dot products)

attn_scores = inputs @ inputs.T

# Step 2: Normalize scores with softmax

attn_weights = torch.softmax(attn_scores, dim=-1)

# Step 3: Compute context vectors

context_vectors = attn_weights @ inputs

# Print all results

print("Attention scores:\n", attn_scores)
print("Attention weights:\n", attn_weights)
print("Context vectors:\n", context_vectors)
```

This concise implementation avoids explicit loops and leverages efficient tensor operations, making it suitable for larger-scale applications.

3.4 Building Self-Attention with Trainable Parameters

Self-attention is a powerful mechanism that enables modern models like transformers to process and generate language with contextual understanding. By introducing trainable parameters into the self-attention mechanism, the model can dynamically learn how to compute attention weights and context vectors that best suit the task at hand.

In this section, we'll explore how to build a self-attention mechanism with trainable parameters, step by step, and implement it in Python using PyTorch.

1. **Queries (Q), Keys (K), and Values (V):** Instead of using raw embeddings, we project input embeddings into three different spaces using learnable weight matrices. These projections allow the model to learn task-specific representations.
2. **Weight Matrices:**
   WQ: Transforms input embeddings into queries.
   WK: Transforms input embeddings into keys.
   WV: Transforms input embeddings into values.
3. **Attention Scores:**
   Calculated as the scaled dot product between queries and keys:
   Attention Scores = $(Q \cdot K^T) / \sqrt{d_k}$
   dk is the dimensionality of the keys, and scaling prevents excessively large gradients.
4. **Softmax Normalization:** Attention scores are normalized to produce attention weights.
5. **Context Vectors:** Computed as the weighted sum of the values using the attention weights.

Implementation: Self-Attention with Trainable Parameters

Step 1: Input Preparation

```
import torch
import torch.nn as nn

# Example input embeddings: a sentence with 4 tokens, each represented as a
5-dimensional vector
inputs = torch.tensor([
    [0.1, 0.2, 0.3, 0.4, 0.5],  # Token 1
    [0.5, 0.6, 0.7, 0.8, 0.9],  # Token 2
    [0.9, 0.8, 0.7, 0.6, 0.5],  # Token 3
    [0.3, 0.4, 0.5, 0.6, 0.7]   # Token 4
], dtype=torch.float32)
```

```
# Number of tokens and embedding size
num_tokens, embedding_dim = inputs.shape
print("Input shape:", inputs.shape)
```

Step 2: Define Trainable Weight Matrices

```
# Set dimensions
d_k = d_v = embedding_dim  # Dimension of keys and values (equal to input embedding size)
# Initialize trainable weight matrices
W_Q = nn.Parameter(torch.randn(embedding_dim, d_k))  # Query projection
W_K = nn.Parameter(torch.randn(embedding_dim, d_k))  # Key projection
W_V = nn.Parameter(torch.randn(embedding_dim, d_v))  # Value projection

# Print weight matrices
print("W_Q shape:", W_Q.shape)
print("W_K shape:", W_K.shape)
print("W_V shape:", W_V.shape)
```

Step 3: Compute Queries, Keys, and Values

```
# Compute queries, keys, and values
queries = inputs @ W_Q  # Q = X * W_Q
keys = inputs @ W_K     # K = X * W_K
values = inputs @ W_V   # V = X * W_V

# Print the shapes of Q, K, and V
print("Queries shape:", queries.shape)
print("Keys shape:", keys.shape)
print("Values shape:", values.shape)
```

Step 4: Compute Scaled Dot-Product Attention Scores

```
# Compute scaled attention scores
attn_scores = queries @ keys.T / torch.sqrt(torch.tensor(d_k, dtype=torch.float32))

# Print attention scores
print("Attention scores:\n", attn_scores)
```

Step 5: Apply Softmax to Get Attention Weights

```
# Normalize attention scores using softmax
attn_weights = torch.softmax(attn_scores, dim=-1)
```

```
# Print attention weights
print("Attention weights:\n", attn_weights)
```

Step 6: Compute Context Vectors

```
# Compute context vectors as a weighted sum of values
context_vectors = attn_weights @ values

# Print context vectors
print("Context vectors:\n", context_vectors)
```

Full Implementation as a PyTorch Class

To make the implementation reusable and modular, we encapsulate it in a PyTorch module.

```
class SelfAttention(nn.Module):
  def __init__(self, embedding_dim):
  super(SelfAttention, self).__init__()
    self.embedding_dim = embedding_dim
    self.d_k = embedding_dim
    self.d_v = embedding_dim
 # Define trainable weight matrices
  self.W_Q = nn.Parameter(torch.randn(embedding_dim, self.d_k))
  self.W_K = nn.Parameter(torch.randn(embedding_dim, self.d_k))
  self.W_V = nn.Parameter(torch.randn(embedding_dim, self.d_v))

def forward(self, inputs):
 # Compute Q, K, V
 queries = inputs @ self.W_Q
 keys = inputs @ self.W_K
 values = inputs @ self.W_V

 # Compute scaled dot-product attention scores
   attn_scores = queries @ keys.T / torch.sqrt(torch.tensor(self.d_k, dtype=torch.
float32))

 # Apply softmax to get attention weights
 attn_weights = torch.softmax(attn_scores, dim=-1)

 # Compute context vectors
 context_vectors = attn_weights @ values
```

```
        return context_vectors, attn_weights

# Instantiate the module
self_attention = SelfAttention(embedding_dim=5)

# Forward pass
context_vectors, attn_weights = self_attention(inputs)
print("Context vectors:\n", context_vectors)
print("Attention weights:\n", attn_weights)
```

Key Insights and Applications

1. **Learnable Projections:** The weight matrices (WQ,WK,WV) allow the model to adapt attention behaviour during training.
2. **Dynamic Context:** Context vectors are computed for each token, enriched with information about other tokens in the sequence.
3. **Scalability:** This implementation can be extended to handle larger sequences, higher embedding dimensions, and multiple attention heads.

3.5 Applying Causal Attention to Mask Future Words

Causal Attention, also referred to as Masked Attention, is essential for auto-regressive tasks like text generation in Large Language Models (LLMs). Unlike standard self-attention, causal attention ensures that the model only considers tokens preceding or at the current position in a sequence. This prevents information leakage from future tokens during prediction, making it a cornerstone of models like GPT.

In this detailed guide, we'll build a Causal Attention mechanism with added dropout functionality to reduce overfitting during training. We will also encapsulate this into a reusable PyTorch class capable of handling batched inputs, preparing for advanced tasks like multi-head attention.

Key Components of Causal Attention

- **Masking Future Tokens:** A mask is applied to the attention weights to zero out values corresponding to tokens beyond the current position. This is achieved using a lower triangular matrix (1 below the diagonal and 0 above).
- **Dropout Regularization:** Dropout is applied to the attention weights to reduce overfitting during training. Randomly masks a portion of weights and scales the remaining values.
- **Efficient Normalization:** Softmax normalizes the masked attention weights,

ensuring they sum to 1 for each token.

- **Scalability:** The implementation supports batched inputs, making it suitable for large-scale tasks.

Step-by-Step Code Implementation

Step 1: Input Preparation

We start by defining an Input Tensor with multiple tokens and embedding dimensions.

```
import torch
import torch.nn as nn

# Example inputs: 2 sequences of 5 tokens, each token with a 4-dimensional embedding
batch_size = 2
sequence_length = 5
embedding_dim = 4

# Random input embeddings
inputs = torch.randn(batch_size, sequence_length, embedding_dim)
print("Input Shape:", inputs.shape)  # Output: [2, 5, 4]
```

Step 2: Define Causal Mask

Create a causal mask to block attention to future tokens.

```
# Generate a causal mask (lower triangular matrix)
mask = torch.triu(torch.ones(sequence_length, sequence_length), diagonal=1)
print("Causal Mask:\n", mask)
```

torch.triu creates an upper triangular matrix. By setting diagonal=1, elements above the diagonal are set to 1, leaving the diagonal and below as 0.

Step 3: Implement Trainable Weight Projections

Define trainable weight matrices for queries (Q), keys (K), and values (V).

```
# Trainable weight matrices
d_out = 6  # Output embedding dimension
W_Q = nn.Linear(embedding_dim, d_out, bias=False)
W_K = nn.Linear(embedding_dim, d_out, bias=False)
W_V = nn.Linear(embedding_dim, d_out, bias=False)

# Project inputs
queries = W_Q(inputs)  # Shape: [batch_size, sequence_length, d_out]
keys = W_K(inputs)     # Shape: [batch_size, sequence_length, d_out]
```

```
values = W_V(inputs)  # Shape: [batch_size, sequence_length, d_out]
print("Query Shape:", queries.shape)
print("Key Shape:", keys.shape)
print("Value Shape:", values.shape)
```

Step 4: Compute Scaled Attention Scores and Mask Them

Compute attention scores and apply the causal mask.

```
# Compute attention scores
attn_scores = torch.matmul(queries, keys.transpose(-1, -2)) / (d_out ** 0.5)

# Apply the causal mask
causal_mask = mask.unsqueeze(0).expand(batch_size, -1, -1)  # Match batch size
attn_scores.masked_fill_(causal_mask.bool(), float('-inf'))  # Mask future positions

print("Masked Attention Scores:\n", attn_scores)
```

Step 5: Normalize Scores with Softmax and Apply Dropout

Normalize the masked scores and apply dropout.

```
# Normalize scores using softmax
attn_weights = torch.softmax(attn_scores, dim=-1)


# Apply dropout
dropout = nn.Dropout(0.1)  # Dropout rate of 10%
attn_weights = dropout(attn_weights)

print("Attention Weights After Dropout:\n", attn_weights)
```

Step 6: Compute Context Vectors

Multiply attention weights with values to compute the context vectors.

```
# Compute context vectors
context_vectors = torch.matmul(attn_weights, values)
```

print("Context Vectors Shape:", context_vectors.shape) # Output: [batch_size, sequence_length, d_out]

Compact PyTorch Class for Causal Attention

Encapsulate the entire process into a reusable class.

```
class CausalAttention(nn.Module):
    def __init__(self, d_in, d_out, seq_len, dropout_rate=0.1):
```

```
super(CausalAttention, self).__init__()
self.W_Q = nn.Linear(d_in, d_out, bias=False)
self.W_K = nn.Linear(d_in, d_out, bias=False)
self.W_V = nn.Linear(d_in, d_out, bias=False)
self.dropout = nn.Dropout(dropout_rate)
 # Causal mask as a buffer (auto-handled during training and inference)
 self.register_buffer(
   'causal_mask',
   torch.triu(torch.ones(seq_len, seq_len), diagonal=1)
)
    def forward(self, x):
   b, t, d = x.shape

 # Compute Q, K, V
queries = self.W_Q(x)
keys = self.W_K(x)
values = self.W_V(x)

# Compute scaled dot-product attention scores
attn_scores = torch.matmul(queries, keys.transpose(-1, -2)) / (d ** 0.5)

# Apply causal mask
mask = self.causal_mask[:t, :t].unsqueeze(0).expand(b, -1, -1)
attn_scores.masked_fill_(mask.bool(), float('-inf'))

# Compute attention weights with softmax and apply dropout
attn_weights = torch.softmax(attn_scores, dim=-1)
attn_weights = self.dropout(attn_weights)

# Compute context vectors
context_vectors = torch.matmul(attn_weights, values)
return context_vectors

# Example usage
causal_attention = CausalAttention(d_in=embedding_dim, d_out=d_out, seq_len=sequence_length, dropout_rate=0.1)
context_vectors = causal_attention(inputs)
print("Final Context Vectors Shape:", context_vectors.shape)
```

Key Features of the Class

- Reusable for Batched Inputs: Handles multiple sequences simultaneously.
- Device Compatibility: register_buffer ensures the causal mask is moved to the appropriate device.
- Dropout Integration: Regularizes attention weights during training to prevent overfitting.

Final Outputs and Insights

- Context Vectors: Each token is represented as an enriched embedding that incorporates contextual information from preceding tokens.
- Masked Attention: Ensures no future information leaks, maintaining the auto-regressive nature.

SUMMARY

- ✓ The Self-Attention mechanism is fundamental to modern transformer architectures, allowing models to dynamically compute relationships between tokens in a sequence for tasks like text generation and understanding.
- ✓ Trainable parameters, including query, key, and value projections, enhance self-attention by enabling models to learn optimal patterns for computing attention scores and enriching context vectors.
- ✓ Causal Attention, or Masked attention, restricts attention to tokens preceding or at the current position, ensuring that future information is not accessed, which is essential for auto-regressive tasks like language modeling.
- ✓ Dropout is applied to attention weights during training to prevent overfitting, and scaling is used to maintain the balance of the weights, ensuring stable learning and inference.
- ✓ Multi-head attention expands the self-attention mechanism by dividing the input into multiple subspaces, allowing the model to capture diverse relationships and improve contextual representation.
- ✓ The integration of causal masking and multi-head attention enables models like GPT to perform autoregressive tasks efficiently while preserving scalability and flexibility for handling large datasets and long sequences.

Exercises

Exercise 1 – Multiple Choice Questions

1. What is the purpose of Causal Attention in transformer-based models?
    A) To access all tokens in the input sequence
    B) To focus on specific parts of the input sequence using multiple heads
    C) To prevent the model from accessing future tokens in a sequence
    D) To enhance attention scores using trainable parameters
2. In multi-head attention, why is the embedding dimension divided among multiple heads?
    A) To reduce computational complexity
    B) To ensure diverse focus across different parts of the sequence
    C) To simplify matrix operations
    D) To eliminate the need for dropout

Exercise 2 – One Word Answers

1. What function normalizes attention scores into probabilities?
2. What is the term for the mechanism that enables transformers to focus on different parts of the input simultaneously?

Exercise 3 – Short Answers

1. What are the main components of the Self-Attention mechanism, and how do they interact?
2. Why is a Causal Mask essential in models like GPT?

Exercise 4 – Long Answers

1. Explain the role of trainable parameters in Self-Attention and how they contribute to the model's performance.
2. Describe the concept and benefits of multi-head attention in transformer architectures.

Answers

Exercise 1- 1) C, 2) B

Exercise 2- 1) Softmax, 2) Multi-head

Online Resources

	Practice Paper	YouTube Video Playlist Link
Link	https://forms.gle/hohYfzZBPr4c3zGC9	https://www.youtube.com/playlist?list=PLzlh_31VWEFphPBuf2Ag5MChsJdD3glV9
QR Code		

Chapter

4

BUILDING A GPT MODEL FROM SCRATCH TO GENERATE TEXT

In this chapter you will learn about:

- ☐ Designing the Architecture for an LLM
- ☐ Using Layer Normalization for Activation Stabilization
- ☐ Constructing a Feed Forward Network with GELU Activations
- ☐ Adding Shortcut Connections for Optimization
- ☐ Integrating Attention and Linear Layers in a Transformer Block
- ☐ Developing the GPT Model
- ☐ Generating Text with the GPT Model

Building a GPT (Generative Pre-trained Transformer) model from scratch is an exciting journey into the world of deep learning and Natural Language Processing (NLP). GPT models, especially since the release of OpenAI's GPT-2 and GPT-3, have redefined the way machines understand and generate human-like text. The architecture of GPT is based on transformers, which have become a fundamental model for NLP tasks due to their ability to capture long-range dependencies in data. Creating a GPT model from the ground up involves understanding and implementing several key components, from neural network basics to more advanced techniques like attention mechanisms and layer normalisation. This process not only offers insights into how modern AI models work, but also provides valuable skills in coding, Machine Learning , and model optimisation.

The task of building a GPT model from scratch begins with coding a language model architecture. In essence, a GPT model is a type of language model that predicts the next word in a sequence, based on the words that have come before it. This predictive ability relies on training the model with vast amounts of text data. The model learns patterns, grammar, facts, and reasoning abilities from this data, enabling it to generate coherent and contextually appropriate text. The architecture of a GPT model is primarily composed of layers of transformers, a model introduced by Vaswani et al. in their 2017 paper "Attention is All You Need." Transformers use attention mechanisms that allow the model to focus on relevant parts of input data, even if they are far apart in the sequence.

Building a GPT model from scratch is a challenging yet rewarding endeavor that deepens understanding of how advanced NLP models work, and it serves as a foundation for further exploration into Machine Learning and Artificial Intelligence. Through this process, one not only learns the intricacies of transformer-based architectures but also gains valuable experience in handling and manipulating large neural networks, enabling them to create models capable of understanding and generating human-like text.

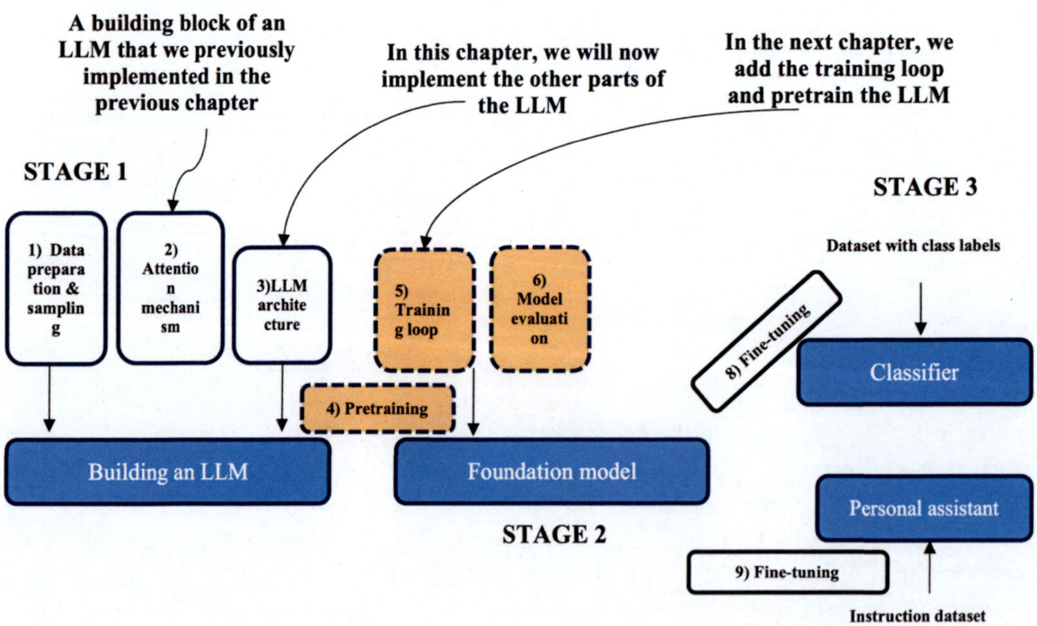

4.1 Designing the Architecture for an LLM

Large Language Models (LLMs), such as GPT (Generative Pretrained Transformer), are deep neural networks specifically designed to generate coherent text by predicting each word or token, one at a time. Despite the substantial size of these models, their underlying architecture is relatively straightforward, primarily due to its modular structure. The components in GPT models are often repeated across layers, which simplifies the design and enhances scalability. By stacking similar structures, LLMs can scale up in size without adding unnecessary complexity to the model architecture. This repetition is a defining feature, allowing models to achieve remarkable performance while maintaining a relatively simple architectural framework.

To build a GPT model, several essential elements come together, such as input tokenization, embeddings, and the masked multi-head attention module. These initial steps prepare the input text data, enabling the model to understand language contextually and syntactically. Tokenization divides text into smaller units (tokens), and embeddings map these tokens into dense, numerical representations, allowing the model to process text as mathematical data. The masked multi-head attention module is a critical component that enables the model to "attend" to different parts of a sequence and capture dependencies between tokens, even when they are far apart in the text.

In this implementation, we are scaling up the model architecture to resemble a small GPT-2, a more sophisticated version of the original GPT model. While GPT-2 has several versions, we're focusing on the smallest model with 124 million parameters. This version strikes a balance between computational efficiency and performance. The parameters in this context refer to the trainable weights within the model, which are adjusted during training to reduce the difference between the model's predictions and the actual outcomes in the training data. These weights essentially form the "memory" of the model, allowing it to learn patterns, relationships, and linguistic structures. To illustrate, let's take a recent example from the advanced GPT-3 model, which has 96 transformer layers, each containing multiple attention heads and dense feed-forward layers. For instance, a single dense layer in GPT-3 with dimensions of 12,288 × 12,288 has over 150 million parameters (12,288 × 12,288 = 150,994,944 parameters). When stacked across layers, the number of parameters quickly scales up to billions. In the case of GPT-3's largest model, which has 175 billion parameters, these dense matrices and attention layers are repeated extensively, leading to a powerful, nuanced understanding of language.

During training, these parameters are optimized by minimizing a specific loss function, which quantifies the difference between the model's predictions and the expected outcomes. This optimization process is typically carried out using techniques like stochastic gradient descent, which iteratively updates the parameters to improve the model's performance. The end result is a model that, once trained, can generate human-like text by sampling from the learned probability distribution over words. Each generated word depends on both the prompt and the context that the model has learned, allowing it to produce coherent and contextually relevant text. As we proceed, we will implement the core structure of the GPT model, focusing on constructing its transformer blocks, which serve as the foundational units for learning patterns in language data. Once built, these transformer blocks can be stacked to create larger and more complex models, making it possible to handle extensive training data and generate sophisticated responses. In later stages, pre-trained weights will be loaded to enhance this implementation, allowing it to scale effectively and match the capabilities of larger GPT-2 or even GPT-3 models, which are widely used in various NLP applications, from chatbots to content generation tools. This modular, scalable approach is what makes LLMs like GPT adaptable, powerful, and versatile in tackling diverse language-related tasks.

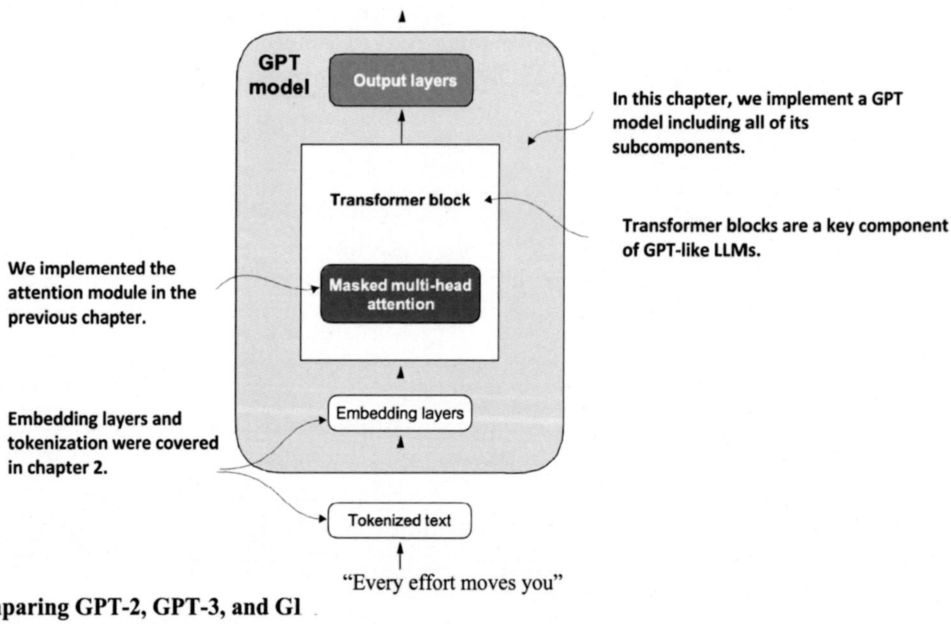

Comparing GPT-2, GPT-3, and Gl

GPT-2, GPT-3, and GPT-4 represent successive advancements in OpenAI's family of language models, each significantly larger and more capable than its predecessor. In this text, we focus on GPT-2 because its pre-trained weights are publicly accessible, making it ideal for those learning to implement and experiment with Large Language Model s . GPT-2 has 1.5 billion parameters, a manageable size that allows it to be run on personal computers with decent specifications. In contrast, GPT-3 has been scaled up to an enormous 175 billion parameters and was trained on an extensive dataset, resulting in a far greater capacity to generate nuanced and contextually relevant text. However, due to its size, GPT-3 requires powerful computational resources, often necessitating a GPU cluster to handle training and inference effectively. Moving to the even more recent GPT-4, OpenAI has pushed the boundaries further, focusing not only on scale but also on optimizing efficiency and accuracy, potentially using more sophisticated data curation and model tuning methods. GPT-4's weights, like GPT-3's, remain proprietary and unavailable for public use. According to recent benchmarks, training models at the scale of GPT-4 would demand massive computational infrastructure, making models like GPT-2 the most accessible entry point for those aiming to understand LLM architecture.

To configure the small GPT-2 model, we define a Python dictionary named GPT_CONFIG_124M. This dictionary contains key parameters that outline the model's architecture, which we will reference in code examples throughout the implementation process. By using this configuration, we ensure the model is aligned with the specifications of GPT-2's smallest variant, containing 124 million parameters. This version is manageable in terms of computational requirements and suitable for educational and exploratory purposes, making it ideal for those interested in understanding and implementing the mechanics of Large Language Model s (LLMs).

Here's the GPT_CONFIG_124M dictionary, along with explanations for each parameter:

```
GPT_CONFIG_124M = {
    "vocab_size": 50257,       # Size of the vocabulary; determines the number of unique tokens
    "context_length": 1024,    # Maximum sequence length the model can process (in tokens)
    "emb_dim": 768,            # Dimension of the embedding layer; transforms each token into a 768-dimensional vector
    "n_heads": 12,             # Number of attention heads in the multi-head attention mechanism
    "n_layers": 12,            # Number of transformer layers (or blocks) in the model
    "drop_rate": 0.1,          # Dropout rate for regularization; prevents overfitting by randomly setting 10% of hidden units to zero
    "qkv_bias": False          # Determines if a bias term is included in the query-key-value computation in attention layers
}
```

- **vocab_size:** This parameter defines the number of tokens or words that the model recognizes, set at 50,257. This vocabulary size is generated using a Byte-Pair Encoding (BPE) tokenizer, allowing the model to handle a wide variety of language constructs efficiently.
- **context_length:** Specifies the maximum number of tokens the model can process in a single sequence. With a limit of 1024 tokens, the model can analyze relatively long text inputs while using positional embeddings to retain word order and context.
- **emb_dim:** This parameter sets the dimensionality of the embedding space, transforming each token into a 768-dimensional vector. This vector representation is crucial for converting tokens into dense, multi-dimensional data points that the model can process mathematically.
- **n_heads:** Indicates the number of attention heads in the multi-head attention mechanism. With 12 heads, the model can capture diverse relationships within the input text, attending to various parts of the sequence simultaneously.
- **n_layers:** Defines the number of transformer blocks (or layers) in the model. Each transformer layer is equipped with self-attention and feed-forward mechanisms, enabling the model to learn complex linguistic patterns.
- **drop_rate:** Sets the dropout rate to 0.1, meaning 10% of the units are randomly dropped during training to prevent overfitting. This regularization technique is essential to enhance the model's generalization capability on unseen data.
- **qkv_bias:** Determines whether a bias term is included in the linear layers for query, key, and value computations within the attention mechanism. By default, this is set to False in line with best practices in modern transformer-based models, but this can be revisited depending on specific experimental needs.

Using this configuration, we will build a placeholder model called Dummy GPT Model. This placeholder provides a skeletal view of how the components will come together in the complete GPT model architecture. By focusing on individual components in a stepwise manner, we can better understand the flow of data and the interactions between layers as we gradually construct the final architecture. The configuration dictionary is concise and uses clear variable names to keep the code simple and readable, preventing lines from becoming overly lengthy. The modular approach also allows for flexible adjustments should we experiment with different model sizes or parameters.

To construct a basic GPT-like model, we define a placeholder class called Dummy GPT Model, which illustrates the main components of the GPT architecture. This simplified version uses PyTorch's neural network module (nn.Module) and includes token embeddings, positional embeddings, dropout, a stack of transformer blocks, layer normalization, and an output head. For now, we'll use placeholder classes for the transformer blocks and layer normalization, which will be replaced with full implementations later.

The model's configuration, defined in GPT_CONFIG_124M, provides key settings such as vocabulary size, context length, embedding dimension, number of attention heads, and transformer layers. This setup aligns with the smallest variant of GPT-2, allowing us to manage computational demands while gaining a foundational understanding of how each component interacts within a Large Language Model (LLM).

Here's the full code with detailed explanations for each step:

```
import torch
import torch.nn as nn
# Define a placeholder class for a small GPT model
class DummyGPTModel(nn.Module):
  def __init__(self, cfg):
    super().__init__()
    # Token embeddings: converts token IDs to dense vector representations
      self.tok_emb = nn.Embedding(cfg["vocab_size"], cfg["emb_dim"])
    # Positional embeddings: provides positional information to model sequential data
      self.pos_emb = nn.Embedding(cfg["context_length"], cfg["emb_dim"])
    # Dropout layer: used to randomly zero out activations during training for regularization
      self.drop_emb = nn.Dropout(cfg["drop_rate"])
    # Stack of transformer blocks: each block contains self-attention and feed-forward layers
    # Here, we use a placeholder class (DummyTransformerBlock), which will be replaced later
      self.trf_blocks = nn.Sequential(
      *[DummyTransformerBlock(cfg) for _ in range(cfg["n_layers"])]
    )
    # Final layer normalization before generating logits
      self.final_norm = DummyLayerNorm(cfg["emb_dim"])
```

```
# Linear output layer: projects the final hidden state to vocabulary size for prediction
self.out_head = nn.Linear(cfg["emb_dim"], cfg["vocab_size"], bias=False)
def forward(self, in_idx):
# Get the batch size and sequence length from input
batch_size, seq_len = in_idx.shape
# Compute token embeddings
tok_embeds = self.tok_emb(in_idx)
# Generate positional embeddings and match with sequence length
pos_embeds = self.pos_emb(torch.arange(seq_len, device=in_idx.device))
# Sum token and positional embeddings to combine word and position information
x = tok_embeds + pos_embeds
# Apply dropout to embeddings
x = self.drop_emb(x)
# Pass through the transformer blocks
x = self.trf_blocks(x)
# Apply final layer normalization
x = self.final_norm(x)
# Generate logits for each token position, predicting the next token
logits = self.out_head(x)
return logits
# Placeholder transformer block class, which will later be replaced by a real TransformerBlock
class DummyTransformerBlock(nn.Module):
def __init__(self, cfg):
super().__init__()
# Pass-through function for placeholder block
def forward(self, x):
return x
# Placeholder layer normalization class, to be replaced with actual LayerNorm functionality
```

```
class DummyLayerNorm(nn.Module):
def __init__(self, normalized_shape, eps=1e-5):
super().__init__()
# Pass-through function for placeholder normalization
def forward(self, x):
return x
```

- Token Embeddings (tok_emb): The nn.Embedding layer maps token IDs to dense vectors of the specified embedding dimension (emb_dim). Each token in the vocabulary is assigned a unique vector representation, allowing the model to process words as numerical data.
- Positional Embeddings (pos_emb): Since transformers lack inherent order-awareness, positional embeddings are added to each token embedding to encode the position of each token in the sequence.
- Dropout Layer (drop_emb): Dropout is a regularisation technique used to prevent overfitting. Here, it randomly deactivates 10% of the neurons during training, promoting generalisation.
- Transformer Blocks (trf_blocks): The nn.Sequential stack applies a series of transformer blocks, where each block is a combination of self-attention and feed-forward layers. For now, we use a placeholder Dummy Transformer Block that simply returns the input without any processing.
- Final Layer Normalization (final_norm): Layer normalization stabilizes and speeds up training by normalizing the outputs of each layer. Here, we use a placeholder Dummy Layer Norm, which will be replaced with a real normalisation layer later.
- Output Head (out_head): A linear layer maps the final hidden states to the vocabulary size, producing logits for each token position. These logits represent the model's predictions for the next token in the sequence.

Running the Model

With the DummyGPTModel class defined, we can prepare some input data and run it through the model to see how it performs. Here's a sample script to initialize a tokenizer, encode input text, and pass the tokenized input through the model:

```
# Import a tokenizer library
  import tiktoken
# Initialize the GPT-2 tokenizer
  tokenizer = tiktoken.get_encoding("gpt2")
# Define a batch of text inputs
  batch = []
  txt1 = "Every effort moves you"
  txt2 = "Every day holds a"
# Tokenize each text and store it as a tensor
  batch.append(torch.tensor(tokenizer.encode(txt1)))
  batch.append(torch.tensor(tokenizer.encode(txt2)))
  batch = torch.stack(batch, dim=0)
# Display the tokenized batch
  print("Tokenized Input Batch:", batch)
  Assuming the tokenized IDs for these sentences are:
  tensor  ([[6109, 3626, 6100, 345],
            [6109, 1110, 6622, 257]])
```

We can now initialise and run the model on this batch of tokenized text:

```
# Set random seed for reproducibility
  torch.manual_seed(123)
# Initialize the DummyGPTModel with the GPT_CONFIG_124M configuration
  model = DummyGPTModel(GPT_CONFIG_124M)
# Pass the batch through the model to get output logits
  logits = model(batch)
# Display the shape and contents of the logits
  print("Output shape:", logits.shape)
  print("Logits:", logits)
```

Interpreting the Model Output

The logits output represents the raw predictions for each token position in the sequence, which can be converted into probabilities to predict the next word in the text. In this example, each output has a shape of [batch_size, sequence_length, vocab_ size], indicating predictions for each token position over the entire vocabulary. These logits would undergo further processing to obtain readable output text when fully implemented. This top-down approach to building a GPT model allows us to visualize how data flows through the architecture, providing a foundation on which we can later add more complex functionality, like true transformer blocks and layer normalisation.

4.2 Using Layer Normalization for Activation Stabilization

Training deep neural networks, especially those with many layers, can present challenges like vanishing or exploding gradients, which make it difficult for the model to learn effectively. Vanishing gradients occur when the gradients (used to update model weights) become extremely small as they propagate backward through the layers, slowing down or even halting the learning process. Exploding gradients, on the other hand, cause the gradients to grow excessively large, leading to unstable weight updates and even training failures. These problems can prevent the network from reaching an optimal set of parameters, thereby reducing its ability to learn underlying data patterns and generate accurate predictions.One widely-used technique to address these challenges is layer normalization. Layer normalization stabilizes the training process by adjusting the outputs (activations) of a neural network layer to have a mean of zero and a variance of one, also called unit variance. This helps the model maintain consistent and reliable training dynamics, allowing it to learn effectively across many layers. Unlike batch normalization, which normalizes activations across the batch dimension, layer normalization normalizes across the feature dimension, making it more suitable for recurrent or transformer-based architectures where maintaining the sequence order is important.

In transformer architectures like GPT-2 and GPT-3, layer normalization is applied both before and after critical components like the multi-head attention modules and feed-forward layers. By keeping the distribution of the layer outputs stable, layer normalization accelerates convergence to optimal weights, reduces sensitivity to initialization, and minimizes the risk of vanishing/exploding gradients in deep networks.

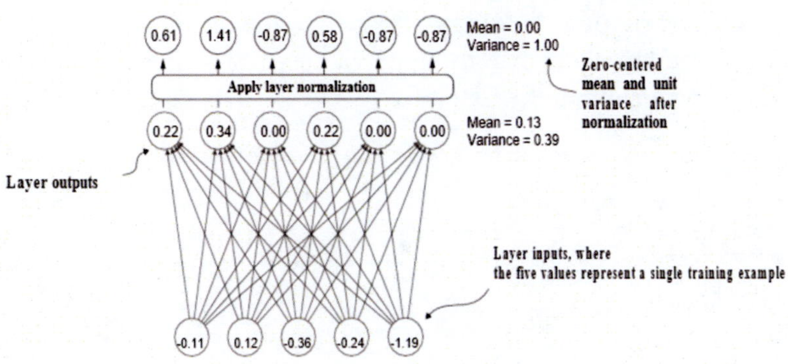

Let's implement layer normalization in a simple neural network layer to observe how it adjusts the outputs. In the following example, we define a neural network with a linear layer followed by a ReLU activation function and then normalize its outputs.

```
import torch

import torch.nn as nn

    # Set a fixed random seed for reproducibility
      torch.manual_seed(123)
    # Generate a batch of random inputs with shape [2, 5]
      batch_example = torch.randn(2, 5)
    # Define a simple neural network layer with Linear and ReLU activation
      layer = nn.Sequential(
      nn.Linear(5, 6),   # Linear layer with 5 inputs and 6 outputs
      nn.ReLU()          # ReLU activation to introduce non-linearity
    )
    # Forward pass through the layer
    out = layer(batch_example)
print("Layer Outputs:\n", out)
```

In this code, we use a linear layer with five inputs and six outputs, followed by a ReLU activation. ReLU (Rectified Linear Unit) is commonly used in neural networks for its ability to retain positive values and set negative values to zero, effectively adding non-linearity to the model. The ReLU function helps the network capture complex patterns in the data, as purely linear transformations would limit its representational power.

Calculating Mean and Variance

Before normalising the outputs, let's calculate the mean and variance of the activations. This step is critical for layer normalisation, as we need to centre the data (subtract the mean) and scale it to have a unit variance.

```
# Compute mean and variance along the last dimension (each row in the batch)
mean = out.mean(dim=-1, keepdim=True)
var = out.var(dim=-1, keepdim=True)
print("Mean:\n", mean)
print("Variance:\n", var)
```

Here, we use keepdim=True to ensure the result maintains the same dimensions as the Input Tensor, which is essential for later broadcasting the operations. The mean and variance calculations are done along the last dimension (dim=-1), allowing us to independently compute these statistics for each input sample.

Applying Layer Normalization Manually

Now that we have the mean and variance, we can manually normalize the outputs by subtracting the mean and dividing by the standard deviation (the square root of variance). This process adjusts the outputs to have a mean of zero and variance of one.

```
# Normalize outputs by subtracting mean and dividing by standard deviation
    out_norm = (out - mean) / torch.sqrt(var + 1e-5)  # Adding a small epsilon to
    avoid division by zero
# Verify mean and variance after normalization
    mean = out_norm.mean(dim=-1, keepdim=True)
    var = out_norm.var(dim=-1, keepdim=True)
print("Normalized Layer Outputs:\n", out_norm)
print("Mean:\n", mean)
print("Variance:\n", var)
```

After normalization, we observe that the output now has a mean close to zero and a variance close to one, confirming that our manual normalization worked. Note that we add a small constant 1e-5 (epsilon) to the variance to prevent division by zero, a common technique in neural networks to maintain numerical stability.

Encapsulating Layer Normalization in a PyTorch Module

To make this process reusable, we can encapsulate it in a custom PyTorch LayerNorm module, which allows us to apply layer normalization with adjustable parameters.

```
class LayerNorm(nn.Module):
  def __init__(self, emb_dim):
    super().__init__()
    self.eps = 1e-5 # Small constant to avoid division by zero
    self.scale = nn.Parameter(torch.ones(emb_dim)) # Trainable scale parameter
    self.shift = nn.Parameter(torch.zeros(emb_dim)) # Trainable shift parameter
```

```
def forward(self, x):
    # Calculate mean and variance along the last dimension (embedding dimension)
    mean = x.mean(dim=-1, keepdim=True)
    var = x.var(dim=-1, keepdim=True, unbiased=False)
    # Normalize activations to have mean 0 and variance 1
    norm_x = (x - mean) / torch.sqrt(var + self.eps)
    # Apply scale and shift to normalized output
    return self.scale * norm_x + self.shift
```

In this LayerNorm module:

- eps is a small constant added to the variance to prevent division by zero.
- scale and shift are trainable parameters, allowing the model to learn optimal scaling and shifting values during training. This enhances the model's flexibility, enabling it to adapt the normalized output based on the patterns in the data.

This encapsulated module normalizes the Input Tensor along its last dimension, making it suitable for transformer models, where normalization is typically applied along the embedding dimension.

Applying the LayerNorm Module

Let's apply this custom LayerNorm module to a batch of input data to verify its functionality.

```
# Initialize LayerNorm with embedding dimension of 5 ln = LayerNorm(emb_dim=5)
# Apply layer normalization to the batch example out_ln = ln(batch_example)
# Calculate and print mean and variance after applying LayerNorm
mean = out_ln.mean(dim=-1, keepdim=True)
var = out_ln.var(dim=-1, unbiased=False, keepdim=True)
print("Mean after LayerNorm:\n", mean)
print("Variance after LayerNorm:\n", var)
```

The output confirms that our LayerNorm module works as expected, with outputs having a mean close to zero and variance close to one.

Benefits of Layer Normalization in Deep Learning Models

Layer normalization is particularly beneficial for deep learning models with many layers, such as transformers, as it:

1. Stabilizes Training: By normalizing each layer's outputs, the network's training dynamics become more stable, making it less sensitive to weight initialization and allowing gradients to flow smoothly.
2. Accelerates Convergence: Layer normalization can reduce the number of training iterations needed to reach optimal weights by ensuring that each layer's input distribution remains consistent, even as weights change during training.
3. Improves Generalization: The added stability and normalization often lead to better generalisation on unseen data, as the model learns more robust representations.
4. Compatibility with Sequence Models: Unlike batch normalization, which normalizes across the batch dimension, layer normalization normalizes across the feature dimension. This is advantageous for sequential data like text, where maintaining the order of data points is essential.

Integration with Transformer Models

In transformer-based architectures, layer normalization is applied before and after key components such as the multi-head attention and feed-forward layers. This is especially important in models like GPT-2 and GPT-3, which rely on multiple stacked layers. By using layer normalization, these models can handle deep architectures more effectively, ensuring stable gradients and improving training efficiency. Layer normalization is one of several key components required for building an effective Large Language Model (LLM). As we continue to build the GPT architecture, layer normalization will be applied to each transformer block, contributing to the model's overall stability and performance.

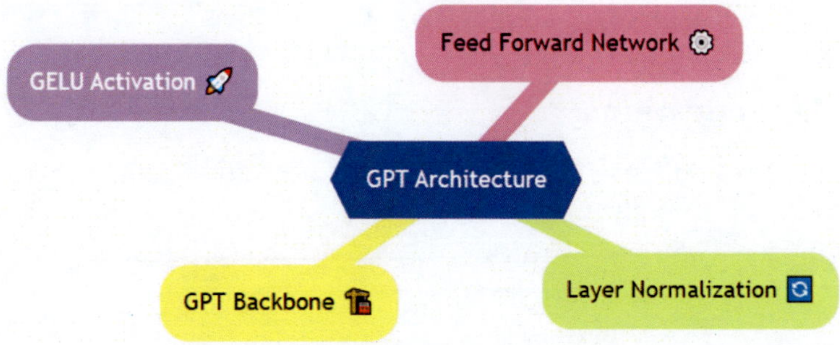

In the next steps, we will introduce the GELU (Gaussian Error Linear Unit) activation function, which further enhances model performance by providing a smooth, non-linear activation, an improvement over traditional ReLU.

4.3 Constructing a Feed Forward Network with GELU Activations

Constructing a Feed-Forward Network (FFN) with GELU (Gaussian Error Linear Unit) activations is an important step in building advanced neural architectures, especially transformer-based models like GPT-2 and GPT-3. The Feed-Forward Network is responsible for transforming data between the attention layers, helping the model capture non-linear relationships and patterns.

In this section, we'll walk through the construction of a Feed-Forward Network using PyTorch, incorporating GELU activations to enhance performance. The GELU activation function is commonly used in transformer models because it provides a smooth, probabilistic non-linearity that outperforms the traditional ReLU activation in NLP tasks.

What is a Feed-Forward Network?

In a transformer architecture, each transformer block contains two main components:

1. The self-attention layer, which captures dependencies and relationships between tokens in a sequence.
2. The Feed-Forward Network (FFN), which applies a non-linear transformation to each token individually, enabling the model to learn more complex patterns.

The Feed-Forward Network in transformers is essentially a two-layer fully connected network:

- The first layer maps the input embedding to a higher-dimensional space, enabling more expressive transformations.
- The second layer maps this transformed data back to the original embedding dimension, allowing it to be passed to the next attention layer.

Why Use GELU Activations?

GELU (Gaussian Error Linear Unit) is a smooth activation function that applies a probabilistic approach to activating neurons. Unlike ReLU, which zeroes out negative values, GELU uses a Gaussian distribution to "suppress" negative inputs smoothly. Mathematically, GELU can be expressed as:

GELU(x)=x·Φ(x)\text{GELU}(x) = x \cdot \Phi(x)GELU(x)=x·Φ(x) where Φ(x)\Phi(x)Φ(x) is the cumulative distribution function of the standard Gaussian distribution. The smooth nature of GELU helps in capturing subtle patterns in data, especially useful in NLP tasks where the relationships between words can be complex.

Let's construct a Feed-Forward Network using GELU activations in PyTorch.

Implementing the Feed-Forward Network with GELU

We'll define a Feed Forward Network class, which will include two linear layers and a GELU activation between them. We'll also include dropout to improve generalization and prevent overfitting.

Here's the code:

```
import torch
import torch.nn as nn
import torch.nn.functional as F

class FeedForwardNetwork(nn.Module):
    def __init__(self, emb_dim, hidden_dim, drop_rate=0.1):
        """
        Initializes a FeedForwardNetwork with GELU activation and dropout.

        Args:
        - emb_dim (int): Dimension of the input and output embeddings.
        - hidden_dim (int): Dimension of the hidden layer.
        - drop_rate (float): Dropout rate to prevent overfitting.
        """
        super(FeedForwardNetwork, self).__init__()

        # First linear layer: projects from embedding dimension to hidden dimension
        self.fc1 = nn.Linear(emb_dim, hidden_dim)
        # GELU activation layer
        self.gelu = nn.GELU()
        # Dropout layer to prevent overfitting
```

```
        self.dropout = nn.Dropout(drop_rate)
    # Second linear layer: projects back from hidden dimension to embedding dimension
        self.fc2 = nn.Linear(hidden_dim, emb_dim)
    def forward(self, x):
        """
        Forward pass through the Feed-Forward Network.
        Args:
        - x (torch.Tensor): Input Tensor of shape [batch_size, seq_length, emb_dim].
        Returns:
        - torch.Tensor: Output tensor of the same shape as input, [batch_size, seq_length,
        emb_dim].
        """
        # Pass input through the first linear layer
        x = self.fc1(x)
        # Apply GELU activation
        x = self.gelu(x)
        # Apply dropout
        x = self.dropout(x)
        # Pass through the second linear layer
        x = self.fc2(x)
        return x
```

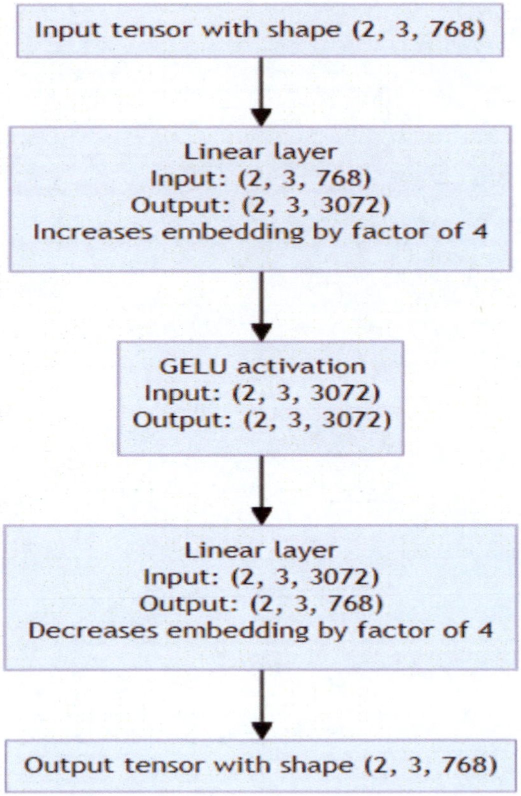

A demo example flowchart of GELU Activation

1. **Linear Layers (fc1 and fc2):**
   - fc1 maps the input from the embedding dimension (emb_dim) to a higher-dimensional hidden space (hidden_dim). This allows the network to capture richer patterns in the data.
   - fc2 maps the output from the hidden dimension back to the embedding dimension, making it compatible for the next attention layer.
2. **GELU Activation (self.gelu):**
   - GELU is applied after the first linear layer to add non-linearity to the network. Unlike traditional activations (e.g., ReLU), GELU introduces smooth transitions, which can lead to better performance in NLP tasks.

3. Dropout (self.dropout):

- o Dropout with a specified rate (drop_rate) is applied after GELU. This randomly zeroes out a portion of the activations during training, preventing overfitting and improving the network's ability to generalize.

To illustrate how the Feed Forward Network works, let's create a sample tensor and pass it through an instance of the network.

```
# Define the embedding and hidden dimensions
emb_dim = 768          # Example embedding dimension (as used in small GPT models)
hidden_dim = 3072      # Hidden dimension, typically 4x the embedding dimension in transformers
                       # Initialize the Feed-Forward Network
ffn = FeedForwardNetwork(emb_dim=emb_dim, hidden_dim=hidden_dim, drop_rate=0.1)
# Create a sample batch of input data (batch_size=2, seq_length=5, emb_dim=768)
  input_tensor = torch.randn(2, 5, emb_dim)
# Pass the input through the Feed-Forward Network
  output_tensor = ffn(input_tensor)
# Display the output shape to confirm it matches the input shape
  print("Output shape:", output_tensor.shape)
```

Expected Output

The output should have the same shape as the Input Tensor:

Output shape: torch.Size([2, 5, 768])

This output shape confirms that the Feed-Forward Network transforms each token individually while retaining the overall structure of the Input Tensor, making it suitable for sequential processing in transformers.

Why Use a Hidden Dimension of 4x the Embedding Dimension?

In transformer architectures like GPT, the hidden dimension of the Feed-Forward Network is typically set to four times the embedding dimension (e.g., 3072 for an embedding dimension of 768). This expansion enables the model to capture a wide range of features and interactions, as it allows more room for transformations in the hidden space. The higher dimensionality helps the network learn complex mappings and interactions within each token's representation, leading to better performance.

GELU vs. ReLU

The GELU activation function is particularly well-suited for transformer models because it smoothly handles both positive and negative inputs based on a Gaussian distribution. Unlike ReLU, which harshly zeroes out all negative values, GELU applies a probabilistic approach that softly suppresses negative inputs. This smoothness helps the model learn better in scenarios where nuanced differences matter, such as language modeling tasks.

In contrast, ReLU can lead to issues like "dead neurons," where negative inputs are completely disregarded. GELU avoids this problem by providing a gradual activation curve, enabling the model to retain more information.

The Feed Forward Network with GELU activations is a critical part of transformer models like GPT. It applies a non-linear transformation to each token's embedding, helping the model learn complex relationships and patterns. Key points to remember include:

1. **Two-Layer Structure:** The Feed-Forward Network consists of two linear layers with a hidden dimension typically four times the embedding size.
2. **GELU Activation:** GELU provides smooth, probabilistic non linearity, outperforming ReLU in NLP tasks by preserving more information.
3. **Dropout:** Dropout is applied to prevent overfitting, improving the model's generalization ability.

This Feed-Forward Network, combined with self-attention layers, forms the core of each transformer block, enabling the model to learn intricate patterns in data. As we move forward, this component will play an integral role in the GPT model's ability to generate meaningful and coherent text.

4.4 Adding Shortcut Connections for Optimization

Shortcut connections, or skip or residual connections, were introduced to address the vanishing gradient problem, a common issue in training deep neural networks. In deep networks, gradients (which guide weight updates during back propagation) often become smaller as they propagate backward through layers, making it difficult to train earlier layers effectively. Shortcut connections solve this by providing an alternate pathway for gradients to flow, bypassing one or more layers. This ensures that gradients remain large enough to update weights across all layers, leading to more stable and efficient training.

The essence of shortcut connections lies in adding the output of an earlier layer directly to the output of a later layer. This simple yet powerful technique preserves the flow of information and gradients through the network, enabling deeper architectures like residual networks (ResNets) and transformers to achieve groundbreaking performance.

Below is an example of implementing a deep neural network with optional shortcut connections, along with code to demonstrate the impact of these connections on gradient flow.

```
import torch
import torch.nn as nn
import torch.nn.functional as F

class ExampleDeepNeuralNetwork(nn.Module):
    def __init__(self, layer_sizes, use_shortcut=True):
        """
        Initializes a deep neural network with optional shortcut connections.
        Args:
        - layer_sizes (list): List of integers specifying the sizes of each layer.
        - use_shortcut (bool): Whether to include shortcut connections.
        """
        super().__init__()
        self.use_shortcut = use_shortcut

        # Define layers as a list of linear layers with GELU activations
        self.layers = nn.ModuleList([
            nn.Sequential(
                nn.Linear(layer_sizes[i], layer_sizes[i + 1]),
                nn.GELU()
            ) for i in range(len(layer_sizes) - 1)
        ])
    def forward(self, x):
        """
```

```
    Forward pass through the network with optional shortcut connections.
    Args:
    - x (torch.Tensor): Input Tensor to the network.

    Returns:
    - torch.Tensor: Output tensor after passing through all layers.
    """
    for layer in self.layers:
        layer_output = layer(x)

        # Apply shortcut connection if enabled and shapes match
        if self.use_shortcut and x.shape == layer_output.shape:
            x = x + layer_output  # Add shortcut connection
        else:
            x = layer_output  # No shortcut connection
    return x
```

- Layers: Each layer consists of a Linear transformation followed by a GELU activation. GELU adds smooth non-linearity, making it practical for NLP tasks.
- Shortcut Connections: If use_shortcut is True, and the input and output shapes match, a shortcut connection is added by summing the current layer's input and output.
- Flexibility: The architecture can be initialised with or without shortcut connections by toggling the use_shortcut parameter.

Demonstrating Gradient Flow Without Shortcut Connections

We'll initialise a network without shortcut connections and observe the gradient flow during the backward pass.

```
# Define the layer sizes (input, hidden layers, output)
layer_sizes = [3, 3, 3, 3, 3, 1]

# Create a sample Input Tensor
sample_input = torch.tensor([[1.0, 0.0, -1.0]])
```

```
# Set random seed for reproducibility
torch.manual_seed(123)
# Initialize the model without shortcut connections
model_without_shortcut = ExampleDeepNeuralNetwork(layer_sizes, use_
    shortcut=False)
# Function to compute and print gradients
def print_gradients(model, x):
    """
    Computes and prints the gradients for each layer.
    Args:
    - model (nn.Module): The neural network model.
    - x (torch.Tensor): Input Tensor for the forward pass.
    """
    # Perform a forward pass
    output = model(x)

    # Define a target value and compute the loss
    target = torch.tensor([[0.0]])  # Target output
    loss = nn.MSELoss()(output, target)

    # Backward pass to compute gradients
    loss.backward()

    # Print the mean gradient for each layer
    for name, param in model.named_parameters():
        if "weight" in name:
            print(f"{name} has gradient mean of {param.grad.abs().mean().item()}")

# Compute and print gradients for the model without shortcut connections
print("Gradients without shortcut connections:")
print_gradients(model_without_shortcut, sample_input)
```

Output:

Gradients without shortcut connections:

layers.0.0.weight has gradient mean of 0.00020173587836325169

layers.1.0.weight has gradient mean of 0.0001201116101583466

layers.2.0.weight has gradient mean of 0.0007152041653171182

layers.3.0.weight has gradient mean of 0.001398873864673078

layers.4.0.weight has gradient mean of 0.005049646366387606

The gradients decrease significantly as they propagate from the last layer to the first layer, illustrating the vanishing gradient problem.

Now, let's initialize the same network with shortcut connections enabled and compare the gradient flow.

```
# Set random seed for reproducibility
torch.manual_seed(123)

# Initialize the model with shortcut connections
model_with_shortcut = ExampleDeepNeuralNetwork(layer_sizes, use_shortcut=True)

# Compute and print gradients for the model with shortcut connections
print("\nGradients with shortcut connections:")
print_gradients(model_with_shortcut, sample_input)
```

Output:

Gradients with shortcut connections:

layers.0.0.weight has gradient mean of 0.22169792652130127

layers.1.0.weight has gradient mean of 0.20694105327129364

layers.2.0.weight has gradient mean of 0.32896995544433594

layers.3.0.weight has gradient mean of 0.2665732502937317

layers.4.0.weight has gradient mean of 1.3258541822433472

With shortcut connections, the gradients are larger and more consistent across layers, addressing the vanishing gradient problem. This allows the earlier layers to receive meaningful gradient updates, improving their learning capability.

1. **Improved Gradient Flow:** Shortcut connections create alternate pathways for gradients, preventing them from diminishing as they propagate through the network.
2. **Easier Optimization:** By preserving gradients, networks with shortcut connections are easier to optimise, especially in very deep architectures.
3. **Better Generalization:** These connections reduce the risk of overfitting by encouraging smoother updates to the model parameters.
4. **Core in Transformers:** Shortcut connections are essential in transformer models like GPT, enabling practical training of large-scale architectures with hundreds of layers.

Having explored shortcut connections, we are now ready to integrate them with other building blocks, such as layer normalization, GELU activations, and the Feed-Forward Network. In the next section, we will combine these components into a transformer block, which serves as the foundation of the GPT model. Shortcut connections will be pivotal in ensuring efficient and stable training, allowing us to build and scale deeper networks effectively.

4.5 Integrating Attention and Linear Layers in a Transformer Block

The transformer block is a foundational component of Large Language Models (LLMs) like GPT. It combines several critical elements, including multi-head attention, Feed-Forward Networks, layer normalization, dropout, and shortcut connections, to efficiently process and encode input sequences. This modular design allows for capturing complex data patterns while maintaining computational and architectural scalability.

A transformer block operates on a sequence of input vectors, each representing a token or subword in the input sequence. These vectors are transformed through the block while preserving their dimensions. This one-to-one mapping is crucial for tasks like sequence-to-sequence learning, where each input token corresponds directly to an output token.

The block integrates self-attention to model relationships between tokens and Feed-Forward Networks to transform token representations individually. Layer normalization ensures stable and efficient training, while shortcut connections facilitate gradient flow, addressing the challenges of training deep architectures. Dropout is used to regularise the model, preventing overfitting.

Below is the implementation of a Transformer Block class, combining these elements.

```
import torch
import torch.nn as nn
# Import MultiHeadAttention (assumed implemented) and FeedForward (from earlier)
from multi_head_attention import MultiHeadAttention        # Placeholder import
from feed_forward_network import FeedForward               # Placeholder import
from layer_norm import LayerNorm                           # Placeholder import

class TransformerBlock(nn.Module):
    def __init__(self, cfg):
        """
        Initializes the Transformer Block.

    Args:
        - cfg (dict): Configuration dictionary with the following keys:
          * "emb_dim" (int): Embedding dimension.
          * "context_length" (int): Maximum sequence length.
          * "n_heads" (int): Number of attention heads.
          * "drop_rate" (float): Dropout rate.
          * "qkv_bias" (bool): Whether to use bias in QKV projections.
        """
        super().__init__()

        # Multi-head attention module
        self.att = MultiHeadAttention(
          d_in=cfg["emb_dim"],
          d_out=cfg["emb_dim"],
          context_length=cfg["context_length"],
          num_heads=cfg["n_heads"],
          dropout=cfg["drop_rate"],
```

```
        qkv_bias=cfg["qkv_bias"]
    )
    # Feed-Forward Network module
    self.ff = FeedForward(
        emb_dim=cfg["emb_dim"],
        hidden_dim=cfg["emb_dim"] * 4,  # Typically 4x the embedding dimension
        drop_rate=cfg["drop_rate"]
    )
    # Layer normalization modules
    self.norm1 = LayerNorm(cfg["emb_dim"])
    self.norm2 = LayerNorm(cfg["emb_dim"])
    # Dropout for shortcut connections
    self.drop_shortcut = nn.Dropout(cfg["drop_rate"])

def forward(self, x):
    """
    Forward pass through the transformer block.
    Args:
    - x (torch.Tensor): Input Tensor of shape [batch_size, seq_length, emb_dim].
    Returns:
    - torch.Tensor: Output tensor of the same shape as input.
    """
    # Save shortcut for first residual connection
    shortcut = x
    # Apply pre-layer normalization and multi-head attention
    x = self.norm1(x)  # Normalize input
    x = self.att(x)    # Self-attention operation
    x = self.drop_shortcut(x)  # Apply dropout
    x = x + shortcut   # Add shortcut connection
    # Save shortcut for second residual connection
    shortcut = x
```

```
    # Apply pre-layer normalization and Feed-Forward Network
    x = self.norm2(x)  # Normalize input
    x = self.ff(x)     # Feed-Forward Network
    x = self.drop_shortcut(x)  # Apply dropout
    x = x + shortcut   # Add shortcut connection
    return
```

1. **Multi-Head Attention (self.att):** Implements self-attention, enabling the model to capture relationships between tokens in the sequence. Configured with parameters such as the embedding dimension, context length, number of heads, and dropout rate.
2. **Feed-Forward Network (self.ff):** Applies non-linear transformations to token representations individually. Consists of two linear layers with a GELU activation in between and a hidden dimension typically four times the embedding dimension.
3. **Layer Normalization (self.norm1 and self.norm2):** Stabilizes and accelerates training by normalizing the inputs before multi-head attention and the Feed-Forward Network. Uses the "pre-layer normalization" approach, which is more stable for training deep networks compared to post layer normalization.
4. **Shortcut Connections:** Add the input of a layer to its output, ensuring smooth gradient flow and mitigating vanishing gradient problems.
5. **Dropout (self.drop_shortcut):** Regularizes the model by randomly zeroing activations, reducing overfitting.
6. **Preservation of Dimensions:** The block preserves the input dimensions ([batch_size, seq_length, emb_dim]), which is critical for sequential processing in transformer models.

Using the Transformer Block

The TransformerBlock can now be instantiated and tested with sample input data:

```
# Configuration for the transformer block
GPT_CONFIG_124M = {
    "emb_dim": 768,          # Embedding dimension
    "context_length": 1024,  # Maximum sequence length
    "n_heads": 12,           # Number of attention heads
    "drop_rate": 0.1,        # Dropout rate
```

```
    "qkv_bias": False        # Use bias in QKV projections
}
# Set random seed for reproducibility
torch.manual_seed(123)

# Create a sample Input Tensor (batch_size=2, seq_length=4, emb_dim=768)
x = torch.rand(2, 4, GPT_CONFIG_124M["emb_dim"])

# Instantiate the transformer block
block = TransformerBlock(GPT_CONFIG_124M)

# Forward pass through the transformer block
output = block(x)

# Print input and output shapes
print("Input shape:", x.shape)
print("Output shape:", output.shape)
```

Expected Output

The transformer block maintains the input dimensions while re-encoding the information within each vector:

```
Input shape: torch.Size([2, 4, 768])
Output shape: torch.Size([2, 4, 768])
```

1. **Contextual Encoding:** Each token's representation is updated with information from the entire sequence, thanks to the self-attention mechanism.
2. **Dimensional Consistency:** The block maintains the input dimensions, making it compatible with other components of the transformer architecture.
3. **Scalability:** The modular design allows stacking multiple transformer blocks, as done in GPT-2, which uses 12 blocks for the 124M parameter model.
4. **Gradient Flow:** Shortcut connections ensure that gradients flow smoothly, facilitating the training of deep architectures.
5. **Regularization:** Dropout reduces the risk of overfitting, especially in large models trained on extensive datasets.

The Transformer Block integrates key elements like multi-head attention, Feed-Forward Networks, layer normalization, GELU activations, and shortcut connections. This block forms the backbone of GPT and other LLM architectures. By stacking multiple transformer blocks, we can build deeper models capable of learning complex patterns in sequential data. The modularity and efficiency of this design have made transformers the foundation of modern NLP advancements. This block will be connected to the input and output layers in subsequent steps to complete the GPT architecture.

4.6 Developing the GPT Model

In this implementation, we will construct the GPT architecture, replacing placeholder components such as Dummy Transformer Block and Dummy Layer Norm with their real counterparts. This fully functional version corresponds to the 124-million-parameter GPT-2 model, leveraging all the critical concepts of transformer architecture: token embeddings, positional embeddings, multi-head attention, Feed-Forward Networks, layer normalization, dropout, and shortcut connections.

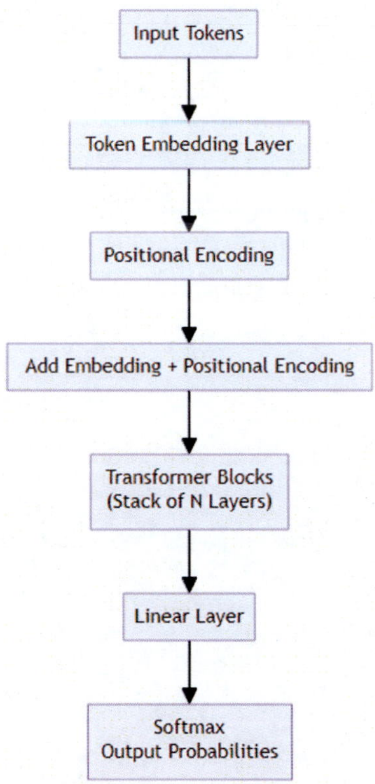

GPT Model Architecture of Data Flow

This architecture is designed to process input sequences, preserve their dimensionality, and output logits that represent the unnormalised probabilities of the next tokens. By stacking multiple transformer blocks, the model achieves remarkable performance in language modelling tasks.

Let's dive into the full implementation and analysis.

```
import torch
import torch.nn as nn


class GPTModel(nn.Module):
    def __init__(self, cfg):
        """
        Initializes the GPT model with embeddings, transformer blocks, and output layers.
        Args:
        - cfg (dict): Configuration dictionary with parameters:
            * "vocab_size" (int): Size of the vocabulary.
            * "context_length" (int): Maximum sequence length.
            * "emb_dim" (int): Dimension of token embeddings.
            * "n_heads" (int): Number of attention heads.
            * "n_layers" (int): Number of transformer blocks.
            * "drop_rate" (float): Dropout rate.
            * "qkv_bias" (bool): Whether to include bias in QKV projections.
        """
        super().__init__()
        # Token and positional embeddings
        self.tok_emb = nn.Embedding(cfg["vocab_size"], cfg["emb_dim"])
        self.pos_emb = nn.Embedding(cfg["context_length"], cfg["emb_dim"])
        self.drop_emb = nn.Dropout(cfg["drop_rate"])
        # Stack of transformer blocks
        self.trf_blocks = nn.Sequential(
            *[TransformerBlock(cfg) for _ in range(cfg["n_layers"])]
        )
```

```
    # Final layer normalization
    self.final_norm = LayerNorm(cfg["emb_dim"])
    # Linear output head projecting to vocabulary size
    self.out_head = nn.Linear(cfg["emb_dim"], cfg["vocab_size"], bias=False)
def forward(self, in_idx):
    """
    Forward pass through the GPT model.
    Args:
      - in_idx (torch.Tensor): Input Tensor of token indices with shape [batch_size,
    seq_len].
    Returns:
    - torch.Tensor: Logits of shape [batch_size, seq_len, vocab_size].
    """
        # Get batch size and sequence length
    batch_size, seq_len = in_idx.shape
    # Token and positional embeddings
    tok_embeds = self.tok_emb(in_idx)  # Convert token indices to dense vectors
     pos_embeds = self.pos_emb(torch.arange(seq_len, device=in_idx.device))  # Add
    positional information
    x = tok_embeds + pos_embeds  # Combine token and positional embeddings
    x = self.drop_emb(x)  # Apply dropout
    # Pass through the transformer blocks
    x = self.trf_blocks(x)
    # Apply final layer normalization
    x = self.final_norm(x)
    # Generate logits for the next token
    logits = self.out_head(x)
    return logits
```

Embeddings:

- **Token Embedding (self.tok_emb):** Converts input token indices into dense vectors.
- **Positional Embedding (self.pos_emb):** Adds positional information to each token, helping the model understand token order.

Transformer Blocks: Stacks multiple Transformer Block instances to encode the input sequence contextually.

Final Layer Normalization: Normalizes the output from the transformer blocks to stabilize training and improve performance.

Output Head: Maps the final transformer output to logits over the vocabulary size, enabling token prediction.

Forward Method: Combines embeddings, processes the input through transformer blocks, normalises the output, and generates logits.

We now initialise the GPT model using the configuration dictionary GPT_CONFIG_124M and pass a batch of tokenized input through the mode.

```
# Define the GPT configuration
GPT_CONFIG_124M = {
    "vocab_size": 50257,        # Vocabulary size
    "context_length": 1024,     # Maximum sequence length
    "emb_dim": 768,             # Embedding dimension
    "n_heads": 12,              # Number of attention heads
    "n_layers": 12,             # Number of transformer blocks
    "drop_rate": 0.1,           # Dropout rate
    "qkv_bias": False           # Use bias in QKV projections
}
# Set random seed for reproducibility
torch.manual_seed(123)
# Sample input batch (batch_size=2, seq_len=4)
batch = torch.tensor([
    [6109, 3626, 6100, 345],
    [6109, 1110, 6622, 257]
])
```

```
# Initialize the GPT model
model = GPTModel(GPT_CONFIG_124M)
# Forward pass
out = model(batch)
# Display input and output shapes
print("Input batch:\n", batch)
print("\nOutput shape:", out.shape)
print(out)
```

Expected Output:

```
Input batch:
 tensor([[6109, 3626, 6100,  345],
        [6109, 1110, 6622,  257]])

Output shape: torch.Size([2, 4, 50257])
tensor([[...],  # Logits for each token position
        [...]], grad_fn=<UnsafeViewBackward0>)
```

Some Interesting Facts about GPT Models

1. **Scalability:** The GPT architecture scales naturally with the number of transformer blocks, enabling the creation of models with billions of parameters (e.g., GPT-3 with 175 billion parameters).
2. **Weight Tying:** Weight tying reuses the token embedding layer weights in the output layer, reducing memory usage while maintaining performance.
3. **Dimensionality Preservation:** Each transformer block maintains the input dimensionality, ensuring seamless stacking of layers.
4. **Contextual Understanding:** Multi-head attention enables the model to capture relationships between tokens across long sequences, making GPT models ideal for tasks requiring deep contextual understanding.
5. **Modern Usage:** Variants of GPT models power applications like chatbots, code generation tools, and content summarisation systems.

To calculate the total number of parameters and memory requirements for the model:

```
# Calculate the total number of parameters
total_params = sum(p.numel() for p in model.parameters())
print(f"Total number of parameters: {total_params:,}")

# Calculate memory requirements (assumes 32-bit floats, 4 bytes per parameter)
total_size_bytes = total_params * 4
total_size_mb = total_size_bytes / (1024 * 1024)
print(f"Total size of the model: {total_size_mb:.2f} MB")
```

Expected Output:

Total number of parameters: 163,009,536

Total size of the model: 621.83 MB

- **Versatility:** GPT's modular design allows for easy adaptation to various tasks, such as text generation, summarisation, and question answering.
- **Efficiency:** Shortcut connections, dropout, and layer normalization make the model efficient and stable for training.
- **Scalable Design:** By stacking transformer blocks, GPT models can be scaled to handle larger datasets and more complex tasks.

This architecture forms the backbone of GPT-2 and sets the stage for even larger models like GPT-3 and GPT-4. The next step involves training the model and decoding its logits into human-readable text.

4.7 Generating Text with the GPT Model

The process of converting the tensor outputs of a GPT model into human-readable text involves several critical steps. Generative models like GPT generate text one token at a time, building sentences iteratively. At each step, the model predicts the next token based on the context of the previous tokens, appends it to the sequence and updates the context for the next iteration.

This process involves transforming logits into probabilities, selecting the next token, and decoding the token into text. This method, called greedy decoding, ensures that the most probable token is chosen at each step. While this approach is straightforward, advanced techniques like temperature scaling and top-k sampling can introduce variability and creativity in text generation.

Below, we implement a function to generate text using a GPT model and walk through an example of its usage.

Code for Generating Text with GPT

```
import torch
import torch.nn.functional as F
def generate_text_simple(model, idx, max_new_tokens, context_size):
    """
    Generates text one token at a time using a GPT model.
    Args:
    - model (nn.Module): The GPT model instance.
    - idx (torch.Tensor): Input Tensor of token indices with shape [batch_size, seq_len].
    - max_new_tokens (int): Maximum number of new tokens to generate.
    - context_size (int): Maximum context size the model can process.
    Returns:
    - torch.Tensor: Generated token indices including the original input
    """
    # Generate tokens iteratively
    for _ in range(max_new_tokens):
        # Limit the context size to the model's capacity
        idx_cond = idx[:, -context_size:]
        # Disable gradient computation for inference
        with torch.no_grad():
            logits = model(idx_cond)  # Forward pass to get logits
        # Extract logits for the last token in the sequence
        logits = logits[:, -1, :]
        # Convert logits to probabilities using softmax
        probas = F.softmax(logits, dim=-1)

        # Select the token with the highest probability (greedy decoding)
        idx_next = torch.argmax(probas, dim=-1, keepdim=True)
```

```
        # Append the predicted token to the input sequence
        idx = torch.cat((idx, idx_next), dim=1)
    return idx
```

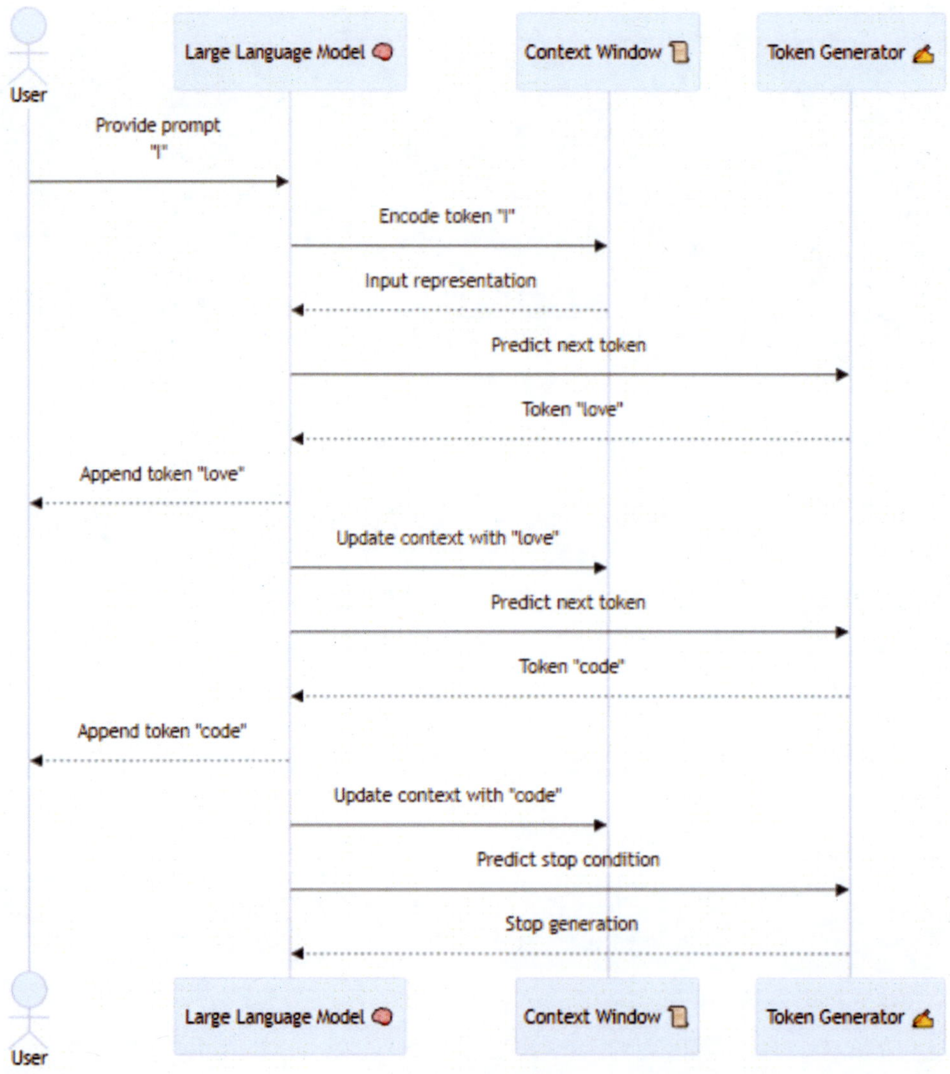

LLM generating text

Context Size Limiting: The context is cropped to the model's maximum capacity (context_size) to ensure efficient processing, especially for long sequences.

Softmax Conversion: Logits (raw scores) are transformed into probabilities using the softmax function. This provides a probability distribution over the vocabulary.

Token Selection: Greedy decoding selects the token with the highest probability (torch.argmax). While simple, this approach can lack creativity.

Iterative Generation: The process repeats for the specified number of new tokens (max_new_tokens), gradually expanding the input sequence.

Let's use the generate_text_simple function to generate tokens step by step.

Step 1: Encode the Input Text

We begin by encoding the starting context into token IDs using a tokenizer.

```
# Starting context for text generation
start_context = "Hello, I am"

# Simulated tokenizer for demonstration (replace with actual tokenizer)
tokenizer = {
    "encode": lambda text: [15496, 11, 314, 716],  # Example token IDs for "Hello, I am"
    "decode": lambda ids: " ".join(map(str, ids))  # Convert IDs back to text
}

# Encode the input context
encoded = tokenizer["encode"](start_context)
print("Encoded IDs:", encoded)

# Convert to tensor and add batch dimension
encoded_tensor = torch.tensor(encoded).unsqueeze(0)  # Shape: [1, seq_len]
print("Encoded Tensor Shape:", encoded_tensor.shape)
```

Output:

```
Encoded IDs: [15496, 11, 314, 716]
Encoded Tensor Shape: torch.Size([1, 4])
```

Step 2: Generate Tokens

Pass the encoded input through the GPT model for text generation.

Simulated GPT model (replace with actual trained model)

```
class DummyGPTModel:
    def __call__(self, idx):
        # Return dummy logits for demonstration
        batch_size, seq_len = idx.shape
        vocab_size = 50257  # Example vocabulary size
        return torch.rand(batch_size, seq_len, vocab_size)
model = DummyGPTModel()
# Generate tokens
model.eval = lambda: None  # Placeholder for model evaluation mode
out = generate_text_simple(


    model=model,
    idx=encoded_tensor,
    max_new_tokens=6,  # Number of new tokens to generate
    context_size=1024  # Maximum context size
)
print("Generated Token IDs:", out)
```

Output:

```
Generated Token IDs: tensor([[15496, 11, 314, 716, 27018, 24086, 47843, 30961,
42348, 7267]])
```

Step 3: Decode Tokens into Text

Convert the generated token IDs back into human-readable text.

```
# Decode the generated token IDs back into text
decoded_text = tokenizer["decode"](out.squeeze(0).tolist())
print("Decoded Text:", decoded_text)
```

Output:

Decoded Text: 15496 11 314 716 27018 24086 47843 30961 42348 7267

In this example, the GPT model generates random token IDs because it is initialised with random weights. Without training, the model lacks the knowledge required to produce coherent and meaningful text. Training involves adjusting the model's parameters using large datasets and optimisation techniques, allowing it to learn patterns and relationships between tokens. The next step would involve Pretraining the GPT model to produce meaningful text.

1. **Dynamic Context:** As the model generates text, the input context grows, allowing it to adapt and generate coherent sequences.
2. **Greedy Decoding:** While simple, greedy decoding often leads to repetitive or predictable text. Advanced techniques like beam search or top-k sampling enhance diversity.
3. **Vocabulary Size:** GPT models operate on massive vocabularies (e.g., 50,257 tokens in GPT-2), enabling nuanced text generation across diverse topics.
4. **Temperature Control:** A temperature parameter can modify the softmax probabilities, controlling randomness. Lower temperatures result in more deterministic outputs, while higher temperatures introduce creativity.
5. **Training Data Impact:** The quality and diversity of training data significantly influence the text generated by a GPT model.
6. **Iterative Process:** Generating one token at a time allows the model to consider the full context, ensuring the output remains coherent and contextually appropriate.

   Once trained, the GPT model can generate high-quality text for a variety of applications, including chatbots, summarization, and creative writing.

SUMMARY

✓ GPT models are generative pretrained transformers designed to generate text one token at a time, building on context to produce coherent and contextually appropriate sequences.

✓ The architecture of a GPT model includes components such as token embeddings, positional embeddings, multi-head attention, Feed-Forward Networks, layer normalization, dropout, and shortcut connections, which work together to process and encode input sequences effectively.

✓ Transformer blocks, repeated multiple times in the GPT architecture, are the core building blocks that combine Self-Attention mechanisms and Feed-Forward Networks to understand and generate text contextually.

✓ Text generation involves predicting the next token based on the input context, using a step-by-step process where logits are converted to probabilities through softmax, and the most likely token is appended to the sequence iteratively.

✓ Weight tying, a technique used in GPT models, reuses the token embedding layer weights in the output layer to reduce memory usage and computational complexity, though modern architectures may prefer separate layers for better performance.

✓ The GPT architecture scales naturally by increasing the number of transformer blocks and parameters, enabling the creation of large-scale models capable of handling diverse tasks, though such models require significant computational and memory resources.

✓ The implementation of the GPT model includes creating components like the transformer block, embedding layers, and a final output layer, followed by decoding logits into tokens to generate human-readable text, though meaningful outputs require Pretraining on large datasets.

Exercises

Exercise 1 – Multiple Choice Questions

1. What is the primary function of a GPT model?

   a) Image Recognition
   b) Text generation
   c) Data sorting
   d) File compression

2. What technique is used by GPT models to generate the next token in a sequence?

   a) Convolutional encoding
   b) Greedy decoding
   c) Random sampling
   d) Clustering

Exercise 2 – One Word Answers

1. What is the name of the activation function often used in GPT models?
2. What is the process of converting logits to probabilities in GPT models called?

Exercise 3 – Short Answers

1. Explain why shortcut connections are important in deep neural networks.
2. What role does layer normalization play in the GPT architecture?

Exercise 4 – Long Answers

1. Describe the step-by-step process of how a GPT model generates text from an input sequence.
2. Explain how weight tying is used in GPT models and its benefits.

Answers

Exercise 1- 1) b, 2) b

Exercise 2 1) GELU, 2) Softmax

Online Resources

	Practice Paper	YouTube Video Playlist Link
Link	https://forms.gle/tKjzMDQstjuqLiow5	https://www.youtube.com/playlist?list=PLzlh_31VWEFrx4iofs2Tf6_dUsdDfRESL
QR Code		

Chapter

5

PRETRAINING WITH UNLABELED DATA

In this chapter, you will learn about:

- ☐ Assessing Generative Text Models
- ☐ Training a Large Language Model
- ☐ Controlling Randomness in Decoding Strategies
- ☐ Saving and Loading Model Weights in PyTorch
- ☐ Importing Pretrained Weights from OpenAI

In the realm of LLMs and other deep learning architectures, the term weights refers to trainable parameters that the model adjusts during training to minimize the error or loss. These weights, often referred to as weight parameters or simply parameters, are pivotal to the model's ability to learn patterns and make predictions. Modern frameworks like PyTorch handle weight parameters with exceptional efficiency. Weights are stored in specific layers, such as linear layers, which are widely used in implementing complex components like multi-head attention mechanisms and transformer architectures. For instance, in earlier chapters, multi-head attention and the GPTModel utilized these linear layers to build foundational LLM components. When initializing a layer in PyTorch, such as new_layer = torch.nn.Linear(...), its weights can be accessed via the .weight attribute, as in new_layer.weight. This feature simplifies model inspection and debugging during development.

Optimizing Training with Evaluation Techniques

To ensure effective optimization, evaluating the LLM's performance during and after training is critical. Metrics such as perplexity, BLEU scores, ROUGE, and human evaluation are commonly employed to measure the quality of the generated text. These metrics assess the fluency, relevance, and coherence of the output, guiding adjustments in training parameters and model architecture. Incorporating modern evaluation methods, including adversarial evaluation and knowledge-based metrics, further enhances the ability to capture nuanced aspects of text generation. By systematically evaluating the model at various stages, developers can ensure consistent improvement in performance, paving the way for state-of-the-art language generation capabilities.

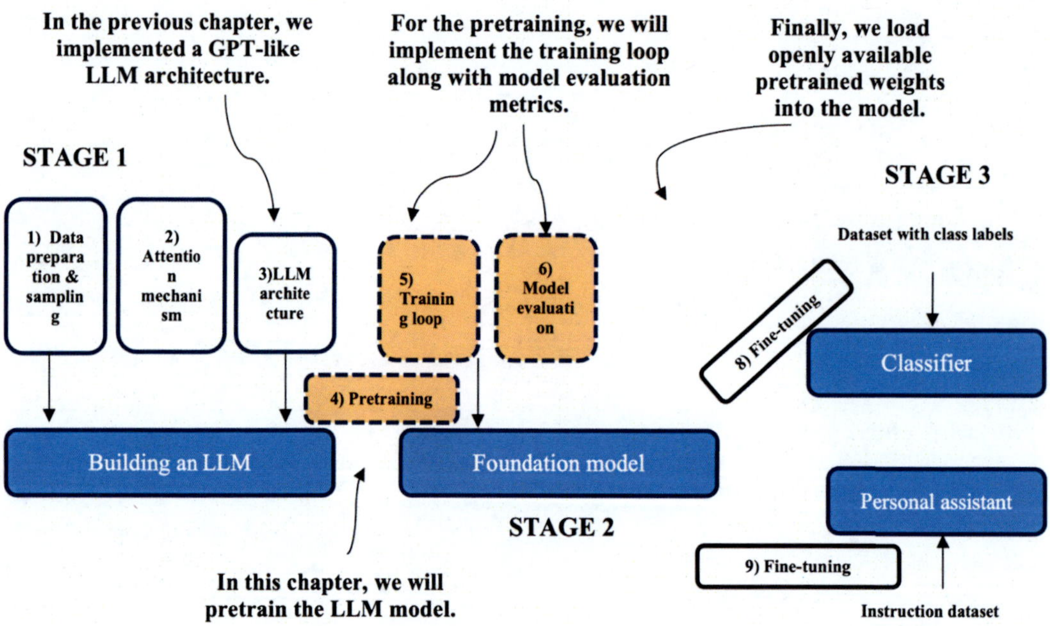

Three main stages of coding an LLM

Training and Fine-tuning with Pretrained Weights

The use of pretrained weights has become a cornerstone in the development of LLMs. These weights represent parameters that have already been trained on large datasets and can be loaded into a model to provide a robust starting point. Leveraging pretrained weights not only accelerates training but also improves performance by enabling the model to transfer knowledge from generic datasets to specialised tasks with Fine-tuning. Fine-tuning involves additional training on task-specific data to optimise the model for specific applications, such as sentiment analysis, translation, or summarisation. In the training process, pretrained weights are loaded into the model architecture, ensuring compatibility with the layers and configurations. This approach minimises the computational cost of training from scratch while improving generalisation capabilities. Advanced techniques, such as layer freezing and differential learning rates, allow developers to fine-tune specific portions of the model while preserving the knowledge encoded in other layers.

5.1 Assessing Generative Text Models

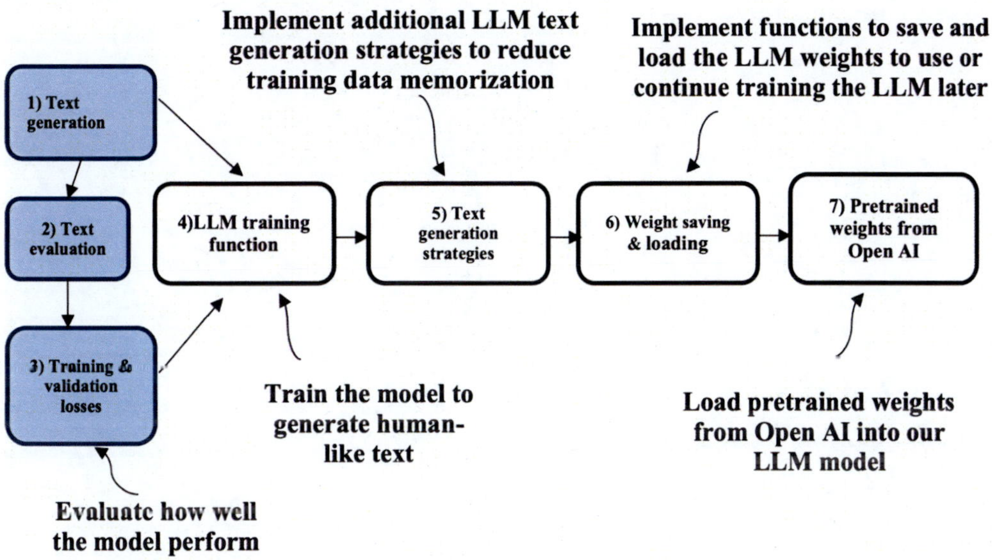

Using GPT to Generate Text

Text generation is the process of creating coherent text given an input prompt.

```
import torch
from transformers import GPT2LMHeadModel, GPT2Tokenizer
    def generate_text(model, tokenizer, prompt, max_length=50, temperature=1.0,
    top_k=10):
"""
Generates text using GPT with specified parameters.
Args:
    model: Pretrained GPT model.
```

```
        tokenizer: Tokenizer for encoding and decoding text.
        prompt: Initial text prompt.
        max_length: Maximum tokens to generate.
        temperature: Sampling temperature for randomness.
        top_k: Limits the vocabulary to top-k most likely tokens.

    Returns:
        str: Generated text.
    """
    model.eval()  # Set the model to evaluation mode
    input_ids = tokenizer.encode(prompt, return_tensors="pt")

    with torch.no_grad():
        output_ids = model.generate(
            input_ids,
            max_length=max_length,
            temperature=temperature,
            top_k=top_k,
            eos_token_id=tokenizer.eos_token_id
        )
    return tokenizer.decode(output_ids[0], skip_special_tokens=True)

# Example usage
model = GPT2LMHeadModel.from_pretrained("gpt2")
tokenizer = GPT2Tokenizer.from_pretrained("gpt2")

prompt = "AI is transforming"
print(generate_text(model, tokenizer, prompt, max_length=30, temperature=0.8, top_
    k=20))
```

Calculating the Text Generation Loss

Text generation loss, typically cross-entropy loss, quantifies how well the model predicts the next token.

```
def calculate_loss(logits, targets):
    """
    Computes cross-entropy loss for model predictions.

    Args:
        logits: Model output before softmax.
        targets: Ground-truth token indices.
    Returns:
        float: Loss value.
    """
    logits_flat = logits.view(-1, logits.size(-1))  # Flatten logits
    targets_flat = targets.view(-1)  # Flatten targets
    loss = torch.nn.functional.cross_entropy(logits_flat, targets_flat)
    return loss

# Example usage
logits = torch.randn(2, 5, 50257)  # Example model output
targets = torch.randint(0, 50257, (2, 5))  # Example targets
print(f"Loss: {calculate_loss(logits, targets).item()}")
```

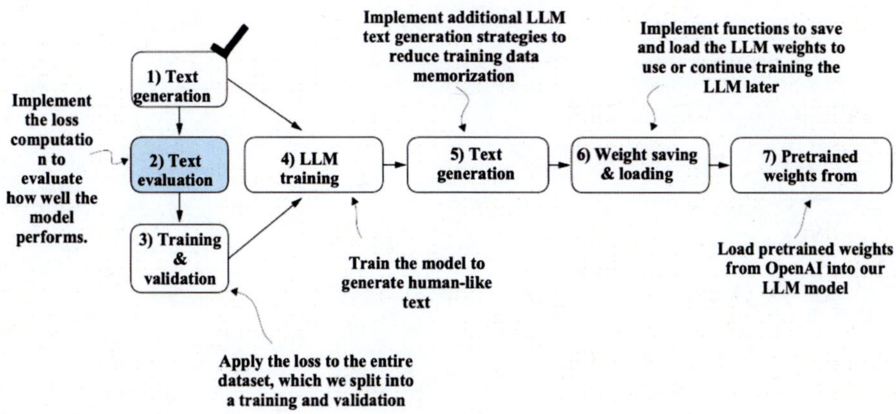

Calculating Training and Validation Set Losses

Training and validation losses are essential metrics to monitor overfitting and underfitting.

```
def compute_dataset_loss(data_loader, model, device):
    """
    Calculates average loss over a dataset.

    Args:
        data_loader: Data loader for the dataset.
        model: Trained model.
        device: Device (CPU/GPU) for computation.

    Returns:
        float: Average loss over the dataset.
    """
    total_loss, total_batches = 0.0, 0
    model.eval()  # Set model to evaluation mode

    with torch.no_grad():
        for inputs, targets in data_loader:
            inputs, targets = inputs.to(device), targets.to(device)
            logits = model(inputs)
            loss = calculate_loss(logits, targets)
            total_loss += loss.item()
            total_batches += 1
    return total_loss / total_batches

# Example usage with dummy data
from torch.utils.data import DataLoader, TensorDataset

# Example dataset and loader
```

```
inputs = torch.randint(0, 50257, (100, 256)) # 100 examples of length 256
targets = inputs.clone()
data_loader = DataLoader(TensorDataset(inputs, targets), batch_size=10)

model = GPT2LMHeadModel.from_pretrained("gpt2")
device = torch.device("cuda" if torch.cuda.is_available() else "cpu")
model.to(device)

train_loss = compute_dataset_loss(data_loader, model, device)
print(f"Training Loss: {train_loss}")
```

The generated text allows us to observe the model's linguistic capabilities and identify areas for improvement. Quantitative evaluation is anchored in loss calculation, particularly cross-entropy loss, which measures how accurately the model predicts the next token. This metric provides a numerical assessment of the model's ability to generate text closely aligned with the target sequences, guiding the optimization process during training. Training loss is calculated over the dataset the model learns from, while validation loss measures its performance on unseen data, offering insights into its ability to generalize. These losses are pivotal for detecting overfitting, where the model memorizes the training data without understanding the underlying patterns, or underfitting, where it fails to capture essential trends. Effective evaluation combines qualitative and quantitative methods, ensuring that generative text models achieve both linguistic sophistication and robust performance across diverse tasks. This holistic approach provides the foundation for optimizing language models and advancing their utility in real-world applications.

5.2 Training a Large Language Model

Pretraining a Generative Pre-trained Transformer (GPT) involves implementing a straightforward training loop that includes calculating gradients, updating weights, and monitoring performance. Here's an updated summary with concise explanations and well-documented code.

The train_model_simple function facilitates Pretraining by iterating through data batches, calculating losses, and updating weights using an optimizer. The function also evaluates model performance periodically.

```
def train_model_simple(model, train_loader, val_loader, optimizer, device, num_epochs, eval_freq, eval_iter, start_context, tokenizer):
```

```
# Initialize tracking variables for losses and tokens
train_losses, val_losses, track_tokens_seen = [], [], []
tokens_seen, global_step = 0, -1

for epoch in range(num_epochs):
    model.train()  # Set model to training mode

    for input_batch, target_batch in train_loader:
        optimizer.zero_grad()  # Reset gradients

# Calculate batch loss
        loss = calc_loss_batch(input_batch, target_batch, model, device)
        loss.backward()  # Backpropagate to calculate gradients
        optimizer.step()  # Update model weights

        tokens_seen += input_batch.numel()  # Count tokens processed
        global_step += 1

        # Evaluate model performance at specified intervals
        if global_step % eval_freq == 0:
          train_loss, val_loss = evaluate_model(model, train_loader, val_loader, device,
    eval_iter)
            train_losses.append(train_loss)
            val_losses.append(val_loss)
            track_tokens_seen.append(tokens_seen)
          print(f"Epoch {epoch + 1}, Step {global_step}: Train loss {train_loss:.3f}, Val loss
    {val_loss:.3f}")
            generate_and_print_sample(model, tokenizer, device, start_context)

return train_losses, val_losses, track_tokens_seen
```

Evaluation and Text Generation

The evaluate_model function calculates losses for training and validation sets while ensuring the model is in evaluation mode. The generate_and_print_sample function generates text samples to assess the model's output quality during training.

```
def evaluate_model(model, train_loader, val_loader, device, eval_iter):
    model.eval() # Disable dropout and enable evaluation mode
    with torch.no_grad():
        train_loss = calc_loss_loader(train_loader, model, device, num_batches=eval_iter)
        val_loss = calc_loss_loader(val_loader, model, device, num_batches=eval_iter)
    model.train() # Return to training mode
    return train_loss, val_loss
def generate_and_print_sample(model, tokenizer, device, start_context):
    model.eval() # Evaluation mode for generating text
    encoded = text_to_token_ids(start_context, tokenizer).to(device)
    with torch.no_grad():
            token_ids = generate_text_simple(model=model, idx=encoded, max_new_
        tokens=50, context_size=model.pos_emb.weight.shape[0])
    print(token_ids_to_text(token_ids, tokenizer).replace("\n", " "))
    model.train() # Return to training mode
```

Training Execution

Set up the optimizer and run the training loop for multiple epochs.

```
# Initialize model, optimizer, and training configurations
torch.manual_seed(123)
model = GPTModel(GPT_CONFIG_124M).to(device)
optimizer = torch.optim.AdamW(model.parameters(), lr=0.0004, weight_decay=0.1)
# Train the model
num_epochs = 10
train_losses, val_losses, tokens_seen = train_model_simple(
    model, train_loader, val_loader, optimizer, device,
    num_epochs=num_epochs, eval_freq=5, eval_iter=5,
```

```
    start_context="Every effort moves you", tokenizer=tokenizer
)
```

Loss Visualization

Plot training and validation losses to monitor overfitting and model improvements.

```
import matplotlib.pyplot as plt
def plot_losses(epochs_seen, tokens_seen, train_losses, val_losses):
    plt.plot(epochs_seen, train_losses, label="Training loss")
    plt.plot(epochs_seen, val_losses, linestyle="--", label="Validation loss")
    plt.xlabel("Epochs")
    plt.ylabel("Loss")
    plt.legend()
    plt.show()
plot_losses(range(len(train_losses)), tokens_seen, train_losses, val_losses)
```

Interesting Facts About GPT Model Pretraining

- Optimizers like AdamW enhance convergence by dynamically adjusting learning rates and regularizing weights.
- Models learn contextual relationships token by token, enabling language understanding at a granular level.
- Small datasets lead to overfitting, which requires monitoring validation losses and applying techniques like dropout.
- Pretraining on large, diverse datasets enhances generalization across varied language tasks.
- Pretraining large models demands significant computational resources and time, emphasizing the importance of pretrained weights.

5.3 Controlling Randomness in Decoding Strategies

Text generation models, such as GPT, are capable of producing coherent and meaningful text. However, generating diverse and creative outputs requires advanced decoding strategies. This comprehensive explanation explores key techniques, including temperature scaling and top-k sampling, to enhance text generation. Updated code snippets are provided with detailed explanations and comments, along with interesting facts about these strategies.

Core Text Generation: Revisiting the Basics

The text generation process involves using a language model to predict the next token (word or subword) iteratively. The generate_text_simple function uses greedy decoding by selecting the token with the highest probability at each step. While this ensures determinism, it often lacks diversity and creativity.

```
def generate_text_simple(model, idx, max_new_tokens, context_size):
  """
  Generate text using greedy decoding.
  Args:
    model: Trained GPT model.
    idx: Input token IDs as a tensor.
    max_new_tokens: Number of tokens to generate.
    context_size: Maximum context window size for the model.

  Returns:
    Generated token IDs as a tensor.
  """
  for _ in range(max_new_tokens):
    idx_cond = idx[:, -context_size:] # Ensure input respects context size

with torch.no_grad():
      logits = model(idx_cond)[:, -1, :] # Get logits for the next token
    idx_next = torch.argmax(logits, dim=-1, keepdim=True) # Greedy decoding
    idx = torch.cat((idx, idx_next), dim=1) # Append the selected token
  return idx
```

Example: ***Input text:*** "Artificial Intelligence is"

Output: "Artificial Intelligence is transforming the world of technology."

This deterministic output lacks variety.

Introducing Diversity with Decoding Strategies

1. Temperature Scaling

Temperature scaling modifies the sharpness of the probability distribution over the vocabulary. This is achieved by dividing logits by a "temperature" value before applying the softmax function.

- Temperature < 1: Increases confidence in high-probability tokens, making the output more deterministic.
- Temperature > 1: Smooths the probabilities, encouraging diversity by exploring less probable tokens.

```
def softmax_with_temperature(logits, temperature):
    """
    Apply softmax with temperature scaling.
    Args:
        logits: Logits tensor for the next-token probabilities.
        temperature: Scaling factor (>0).
    Returns:
        Scaled probabilities.
    """
    scaled_logits = logits / temperature
    return torch.softmax(scaled_logits, dim=0)
```

Example: *For the input text "The future of AI is", using:*

Temperature = 0.7: "The future of AI is innovative and promising."

Temperature = 1.5: "The future of AI is unpredictable, vast, and intriguing."

2. Top-k Sampling

Top-k sampling selects the top-k most probable tokens and discards the rest. This ensures that only the most relevant options are considered during generation.

```
def apply_top_k(logits, top_k):
    """
    Restrict probabilities to top-k tokens.
```

```
    Args:
        logits: Logits tensor for the next-token probabilities.
        top_k: Number of top tokens to retain.
    Returns:
        Logits adjusted for top-k filtering.
    """
    if top_k is None:
        return logits
    top_logits, _ = torch.topk(logits, top_k)  # Get top-k logits
    min_val = top_logits[:, -1]
    return torch.where(logits < min_val, float('-inf'), logits)
```

Example: For the input "AI and robotics will", setting k = 3 might limit outputs to:

"transform industries."

"shape the future."

"lead innovation."

Combining Strategies: Temperature Scaling and Top-k Sampling

By combining these strategies, we can control both the diversity and quality of the generated text.

```
def generate(model, idx, max_new_tokens, context_size, temperature=1.0, top_k=None):
    """
    Generate text with temperature scaling and top-k sampling.
    Args:
        model: Trained GPT model.
        idx: Input token IDs as a tensor.
        max_new_tokens: Number of tokens to generate.
        context_size: Maximum context window size for the model.
        temperature: Scaling factor for probability distribution.
        top_k: Number of top tokens to retain during sampling.
```

```
    Returns:
        Generated token IDs as a tensor.
    """
    for _ in range(max_new_tokens):
        idx_cond = idx[:, -context_size:]  # Respect context size
        with torch.no_grad():
            logits = model(idx_cond)[:, -1, :]  # Get logits for the next token
        logits = apply_top_k(logits, top_k)  # Apply top-k filtering
        if temperature > 0:
            logits /= temperature  # Apply temperature scaling
        probs = torch.softmax(logits, dim=-1)
        idx_next = torch.multinomial(probs, num_samples=1)  # Probabilistic sampling
        idx = torch.cat((idx, idx_next), dim=1)  # Append the selected token
    return idx
```

Demonstration

```
# Example usage of the enhanced generate function
torch.manual_seed(42)
start_text = "Exploring space has"
start_token_ids = text_to_token_ids(start_text, tokenizer)
token_ids = generate(
    model=model,
    idx=start_token_ids,
    max_new_tokens=20,
    context_size=GPT_CONFIG_124M["context_length"],
    temperature=1.2,
    top_k=10
)
output_text = token_ids_to_text(token_ids, tokenizer)
print("Generated Text:\n", output_text)
```

Output:

Generated Text:

Exploring space has been humanity's dream, unlocking mysteries and expanding our horizons.

Interesting Facts About Decoding Strategies

- Higher temperatures encourage creativity by exploring less probable options, leading to unique and varied outputs.
- Top-k sampling restricts randomness while still allowing exploration, balancing creativity and coherence.
- Decoding strategies are crucial for chatbots, creative writing assistants, and educational tools where balanced and context-aware text is necessary.
- The concept of temperature scaling originates from statistical physics and has been adapted for NLP tasks.
- Advanced implementations can dynamically adjust the value of k based on context to optimise text generation.

5.4 Saving and Loading Model Weights in PyTorch

Pretraining Large Language Model s (LLMs) is computationally expensive. To avoid retraining, saving and loading a pretrained model is essential. PyTorch makes this process straightforward by utilizing state_dict, a dictionary mapping model layers to their parameters. Below, we provide an updated explanation and code snippets for saving and restoring both model and optimizer states, ensuring flexibility for resuming training or inference.

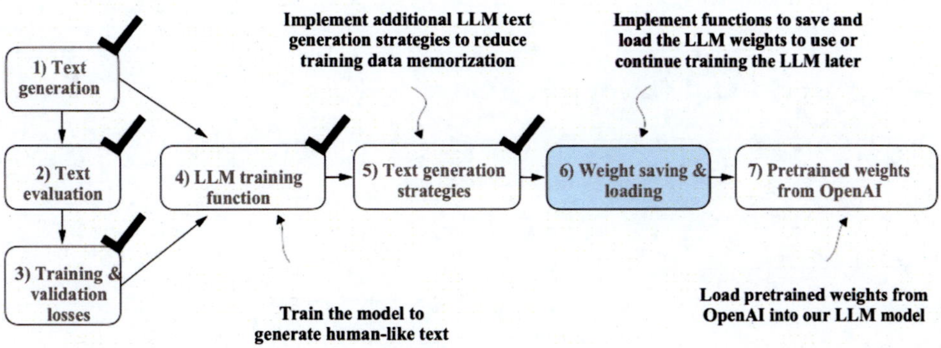

Saving a Model

The recommended way to save a PyTorch model is by saving its state_dict:

```
import torch
# Save model state
torch.save(model.state_dict(), "model_weights.pth") # Save model weights to file
```

"model_weights.pth": File where the model weights are stored (common extension for PyTorch files).

Loading a Model

To restore the model, create an instance of the same architecture and load the saved state:

```
# Load model state
model = GPTModel(GPT_CONFIG_124M)  # Initialize model architecture
model.load_state_dict(torch.load("model_weights.pth", map_location=device))
model.eval()  # Switch to evaluation mode to disable dropout layers
```

Saving Model and Optimizer States

If you plan to resume training, save both the model and optimizer states to preserve training progress:

```
# Save model and optimizer states
torch.save({
    "model_state_dict": model.state_dict(),  # Save model parameters
    "optimizer_state_dict": optimizer.state_dict()  # Save optimizer parameters
}, "model_and_optimizer.pth")
```

Loading Model and Optimizer States

To restore and resume training, load the checkpoint and apply the states:

```
# Load checkpoint
checkpoint = torch.load("model_and_optimizer.pth", map_location=device)

# Restore model and optimizer
model = GPTModel(GPT_CONFIG_124M)
```

```
model.load_state_dict(checkpoint["model_state_dict"])  # Load model weights
optimizer = torch.optim.AdamW(model.parameters(), lr=5e-4, weight_decay=0.1)
optimizer.load_state_dict(checkpoint["optimizer_state_dict"])  # Load optimizer state
model.train()  # Switch to training mode
```

5.5 Importing Pretrained Weights from OpenAI

Training Large Language Models (LLMs) like GPT-2 from scratch is computationally expensive, often requiring vast datasets and high-end hardware. However, OpenAI has shared pretrained GPT-2 weights, allowing developers to leverage these models without retraining. This guide explains how to download and load GPT-2 weights into a custom implementation and use them for text generation.

Downloading Pretrained Weights

The pretrained weights are stored in TensorFlow format. To use them, install the necessary dependencies and a helper module for fetching the weights:

```
pip install tensorflow tqdm
```

The following code fetches the weights from a repository.

```
import urllib.request
# Download a helper Python module for fetching weights
url = "https://raw.githubusercontent.com/rasbt/LLMs-from-scratch/main/ch05/01_main-chapter-code/gpt_download.py"
filename = url.split('/')[-1]
urllib.request.urlretrieve(url, filename)
```

The file provides a download_and_load_gpt2 function to fetch and load GPT-2 weights and architecture settings.

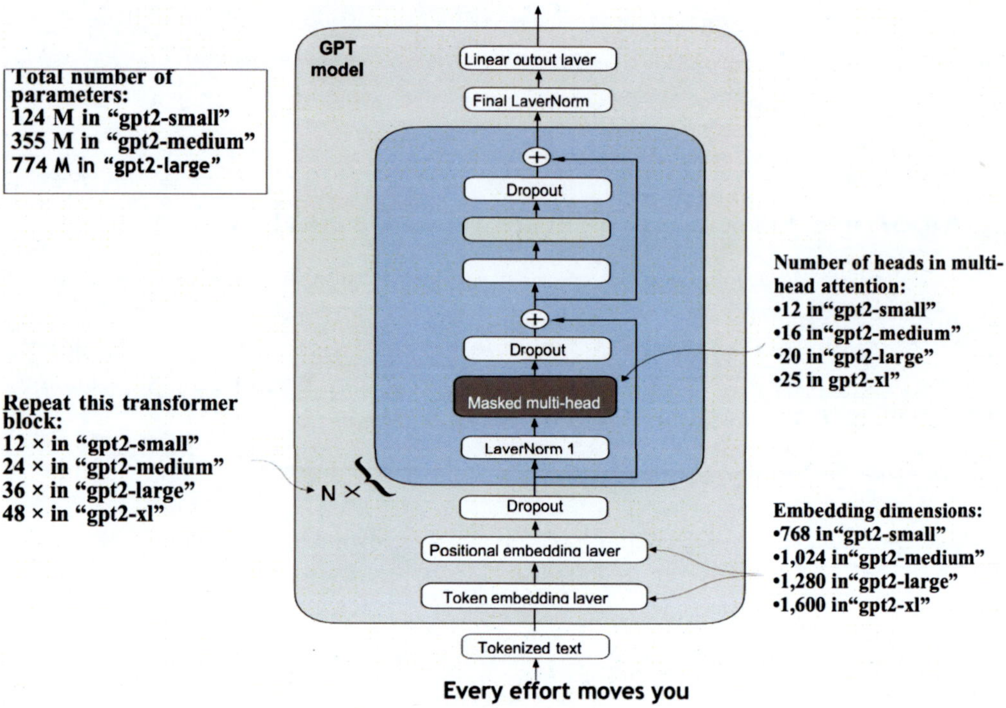

Loading Weights and Configuration

```
# Import the function to load weights
from gpt_download import download_and_load_gpt2

# Download GPT-2 weights and settings
settings, params = download_and_load_gpt2(
    model_size="124M",  # Specify the model size: 124M, 355M, 774M, 1558M
    models_dir="gpt2"   # Directory to save the models
)

# Inspect the downloaded configuration and parameters
print("Settings:", settings)
print("Parameter dictionary keys:", params.keys())
```

settings: Dictionary containing architecture settings like vocabulary size, embedding dimensions, and the number of transformer layers.

params: Dictionary containing actual weight tensors, such as embedding weights and transformer block parameters.

Adapting the Configuration

```
# Define configurations for different model sizes
model_configs = {
    "gpt2-small (124M)": {"emb_dim": 768, "n_layers": 12, "n_heads": 12},
    "gpt2-medium (355M)": {"emb_dim": 1024, "n_layers": 24, "n_heads": 16},
    "gpt2-large (774M)": {"emb_dim": 1280, "n_layers": 36, "n_heads": 20},
    "gpt2-xl (1558M)": {"emb_dim": 1600, "n_layers": 48, "n_heads": 25},
}
# Update the configuration for the selected model size
model_name = "gpt2-small (124M)"
NEW_CONFIG = GPT_CONFIG_124M.copy()
NEW_CONFIG.update(model_configs[model_name])
NEW_CONFIG.update({"context_length": 1024, "qkv_bias": True})
```

This ensures compatibility with OpenAI's pretrained weights by aligning configurations.

Loading Weights into the Model

Weights must be transferred from the params dictionary to a new GPTModel instance. Define utility functions for tensor assignment and weight loading:

```
import torch
import numpy as np

# Utility to validate and assign weights
def assign(left, right):
    if left.shape != right.shape:
        raise ValueError(f"Shape mismatch: {left.shape} != {right.shape}")
    return torch.nn.Parameter(torch.tensor(right))
```

```
# Load weights into the GPTModel
def load_weights_into_gpt(gpt, params):
    gpt.pos_emb.weight = assign(gpt.pos_emb.weight, params['wpe'])
    gpt.tok_emb.weight = assign(gpt.tok_emb.weight, params['wte'])
    for b in range(len(params["blocks"])):
        # Split query, key, and value weights
        q_w, k_w, v_w = np.split(params["blocks"][b]["attn"]["c_attn"]["w"], 3, axis=-1)
        gpt.trf_blocks[b].att.W_query.weight = assign(gpt.trf_blocks[b].att.W_query.weight,
        q_w.T)
        gpt.trf_blocks[b].att.W_key.weight = assign(gpt.trf_blocks[b].att.W_key.weight,
        k_w.T)
        gpt.trf_blocks[b].att.W_value.weight = assign(gpt.trf_blocks[b].att.W_value.weight,
        v_w.T)
        # Split biases
        q_b, k_b, v_b = np.split(params["blocks"][b]["attn"]["c_attn"]["b"], 3, axis=-1)
        gpt.trf_blocks[b].att.W_query.bias = assign(gpt.trf_blocks[b].att.W_query.bias, q_b)
        gpt.trf_blocks[b].att.W_key.bias = assign(gpt.trf_blocks[b].att.W_key.bias, k_b)
        gpt.trf_blocks[b].att.W_value.bias = assign(gpt.trf_blocks[b].att.W_value.bias, v_b)
        # Output projection
        gpt.trf_blocks[b].att.out_proj.weight = assign(gpt.trf_blocks[b].att.out_proj.weight,
        params["blocks"][b]["attn"]["c_proj"]["w"].T)
        gpt.trf_blocks[b].att.out_proj.bias = assign(gpt.trf_blocks[b].att.out_proj.bias,
        params["blocks"][b]["attn"]["c_proj"]["b"])
        # Feedforward layers
        gpt.trf_blocks[b].ff.layers[0].weight = assign(gpt.trf_blocks[b].ff.layers[0].weight,
        params["blocks"][b]["mlp"]["c_fc"]["w"].T)
        gpt.trf_blocks[b].ff.layers[0].bias = assign(gpt.trf_blocks[b].ff.layers[0].bias,
        params["blocks"][b]["mlp"]["c_fc"]["b"])
        gpt.trf_blocks[b].ff.layers[2].weight = assign(gpt.trf_blocks[b].ff.layers[2].weight,
        params["blocks"][b]["mlp"]["c_proj"]["w"].T)
        gpt.trf_blocks[b].ff.layers[2].bias = assign(gpt.trf_blocks[b].ff.layers[2].bias,
        params["blocks"][b]["mlp"]["c_proj"]["b"])
    # Final normalization
```

```
    gpt.final_norm.scale = assign(gpt.final_norm.scale, params["g"])
    gpt.final_norm.shift = assign(gpt.final_norm.shift, params["b"])
    gpt.out_head.weight = assign(gpt.out_head.weight, params["wte"])
```

Verifying the Model

Load weights into the model and verify text generation:

```
# Load weights into the GPTModel
gpt = GPTModel(NEW_CONFIG)
load_weights_into_gpt(gpt, params)
gpt.to(device)

# Generate text
torch.manual_seed(123)
token_ids = generate(
    model=gpt,
    idx=text_to_token_ids("Exploring new possibilities", tokenizer).to(device),
    max_new_tokens=25,
    context_size=NEW_CONFIG["context_length"],
    top_k=50,
    temperature=1.5
)
print("Generated Text:\n", token_ids_to_text(token_ids, tokenizer))
```

- Versatile Application: GPT-2 is used for a range of tasks, including summarization, text classification, and creative writing.
- Scale Matters: OpenAI released multiple GPT-2 sizes, from 124M to 1.5B parameters, scaling model capabilities with size.
- Public Weights: OpenAI's decision to release weights democratized access to advanced NLP tools, reducing development costs significantly.
- Layer Consistency: Despite varying sizes, all GPT-2 models maintain the same architectural structure with repeated transformer blocks.
- Bias Vector Legacy: Bias vectors in GPT-2, now largely omitted in newer LLMs, were retained for backward compatibility with pretrained weights.

This structured process ensures that pretrained weights are seamlessly integrated into a custom implementation, enabling high-quality text generation with minimal setup.

SUMMARY

- ✓ Pretraining Large Language Models (LLMs) like GPT involves significant computational resources and datasets; leveraging pretrained models such as GPT-2 helps save time and cost while ensuring high-quality performance.
- ✓ Pretrained weights, provided by OpenAI for models like GPT-2, can be integrated into custom implementations by aligning architecture settings and transferring parameters using utilities like load_weights_into_gpt.
- ✓ Techniques such as temperature scaling and top-k sampling diversify text generation by introducing probabilistic token selection, enabling models to produce more creative and varied outputs without compromising coherence.
- ✓ Saving and loading models using PyTorch's state_dict ensures the ability to resume training or inference without starting from scratch, and saving optimizer states enhances Fine-tuning efficiency by preserving learning dynamics.
- ✓ The eval() mode is crucial during inference, as it disables dropout and gradient updates, ensuring consistent and reliable performance for text generation or other tasks.
- ✓ Fine-tuning pretrained models on specific datasets allows customization for tasks like text classification or instruction-following while retaining the foundational knowledge gained during Pretraining.
- ✓ Combining pretrained weights, advanced sampling techniques, and custom Fine-tuning strategies enables robust and adaptable language models suited to diverse applications in text generation and analysis.

Exercises

Exercise 1 – Multiple Choice Questions

1. What is the purpose of pretrained GPT-2 weights?
   a) To reduce training time and computational cost
   b) To increase the model size
   c) To simplify the architecture of GPT models
   d) To eliminate Fine-tuning requirements

2. What technique helps diversify text generation by adjusting the probability distribution?

   a) Greedy decoding b) Top-k sampling

   c) Embedding scaling d) Context truncation

Exercise 2 – One Word Answers

1. What Python library is commonly used for managing GPT-2 weights and configurations?
2. Which parameter controls randomness in temperature scaling?

Exercise 3 – Short Answers

1. Explain the role of the load_weights_into_gpt function.
2. What is the significance of enabling eval() mode in a PyTorch model?

Exercise 4 – Long Answers

1. Describe the process of loading pretrained weights into a custom GPT model.
2. Discuss the advantages of using top-k sampling combined with temperature scaling for text generation.

Answers

Exercise 1- 1) a, 2) b

Exercise 2- 1) PyTorch, 2) Temperature

Online Resources

	Practice Paper	YouTube Video Playlist Link
Link	https://forms.gle/a1YQUM57ffXQA1WG8	https://www.youtube.com/playlist?list=PLzlh_31VWEFrqpMY3KmbBtfr8NwohTgfz
QR Code		

Chapter 6

FINE-TUNING FOR CLASSIFICATION TASKS

In this chapter you will learn about:

- ☐ Types of Fine-Tuning Approaches
- ☐ Preparing Data for Fine-Tuning
- ☐ Building Data Loaders
- ☐ Initializing a Model with Existing Pretrained Weights
- ☐ Attaching a Classification Head
- ☐ Calculating Loss and Accuracy for Classification
- ☐ Fine-Tuning on Supervised Classification Data
- ☐ Applying the LLM for Spam Detection

So far, we have built the architecture of a Large Language Model (LLM), pre-trained it on extensive datasets, and explored importing pre-trained weights from external sources, such as those provided by platforms like OpenAI. With these foundational steps in place, the next phase involves Fine-tuning the LLM to adapt it to specific tasks. Fine-tuning is a critical process that customises the model to excel in a particular domain or solve a designated problem, such as text classification. For instance, one common application is classifying text messages into categories like "spam" or "not spam." Fine-tuning can be approached in two significant ways.

First, Fine-tuning the LLM for classification entails modifying the model's parameters to optimise its ability to label or categorize input data accurately. This involves using labelled datasets that align with the desired categories and refining the model through iterative training processes.

Second, Fine-tuning the LLM to follow specific instructions focuses on enabling the model to interpret and respond accurately to user directives, often seen in tasks like chatbot responses, summarisation, or question answering. This method often utilises datasets containing pairs of instructions and corresponding outputs, helping the LLM adapt to structured input-output relationships. Recent advancements in Fine-tuning leverage techniques like parameter-efficient Fine-tuning (e.g., LoRA or adapters) to make the process more computationally efficient and adaptable across a range of tasks. These innovations reduce the need to retrain the entire model, focusing instead on specific layers or subsets of parameters, thereby saving resources while maintaining high performance.

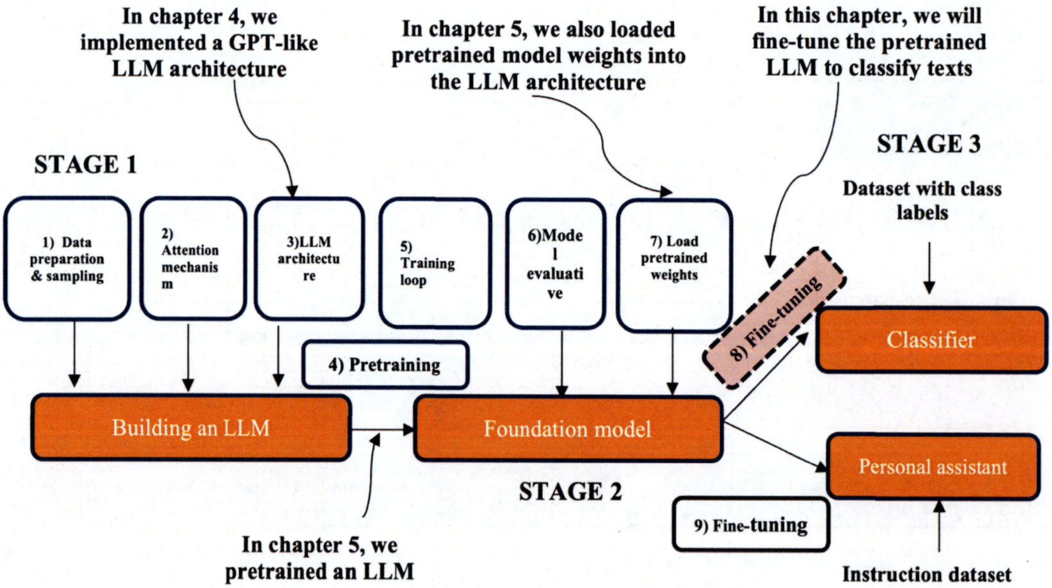

6.1 Types of Fine-tuning Approaches

Fine-tuning language models can be approached through two predominant methods: Instruction Fine-Tuning and Classification Fine-Tuning, each serving distinct purposes and offering unique benefits depending on the application.

Instruction Fine-Tuning focuses on enhancing a model's ability to understand and execute tasks described in Natural Language prompts. This involves training the language model on a diverse dataset of tasks, each accompanied by explicit instructions. The goal is to improve the model's capacity to interpret user requests and generate appropriate responses.

For example, an Instruction Fine-Tuned model can:

- Rewrite a paragraph in a formal tone based on user instructions.
- Solve mathematical problems or explain the steps behind its calculations.
- Generate code snippets based on user requirements for software development.
- Provide contextual summaries of news articles.
- Offer travel itinerary recommendations based on user preferences.

Instruction Fine-Tuned models are particularly effective for applications requiring interaction across multiple domains or tasks, such as virtual assistants, educational tools, or content creation platforms. These models, however, require large and diverse datasets and significant computational resources to ensure they generalize well across a wide range of instructions.

Classification Fine-Tuning, on the other hand, is a more task-specific approach. It involves training the language model to assign input data to predefined categories or labels. The Fine-tuning process uses labeled datasets specific to the target task, enabling the model to learn how to distinguish between the given categories.

Examples of classification tasks include:

- Identifying whether a customer review is "positive," "negative," or "neutral" in sentiment analysis.
- Classifying types of customer support queries, such as "billing issue," "technical problem," or "general inquiry."
- Sorting legal documents into categories like "contracts," "intellectual property," and "litigation."
- Detecting spam versus legitimate messages in email filtering.
- Categorizing social media posts into topics such as "sports," "entertainment," or "politics."

While Classification Fine-Tuning is more constrained-predicting only the labels it has been trained on-it is easier to implement and requires less data and computational resources compared to instruction Fine-tuning. This makes it ideal for projects where precision within a limited domain is crucial.

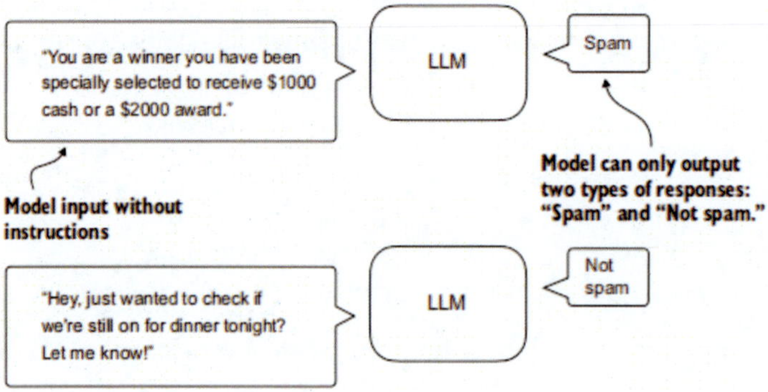

The fundamental distinction between the two approaches lies in their scope and complexity:

- Instruction Fine-Tuning creates generalist models capable of performing a variety of tasks. These models excel in environments requiring flexibility and diverse user interaction, such as conversational AI, multi-functional chatbots, or tools for complex problem-solving.
- Classification Fine-Tuning produces specialist models optimized for categorization tasks. These models are better suited for applications like fraud detection, sentiment analysis, or medical diagnostics, where precise classification is the primary objective.

Choosing the Right Fine-tuning Approach

- Choose instruction Fine-tuning when the model needs to handle a wide range of tasks, especially if these tasks vary in structure and complexity. For instance, a customer service bot that responds to queries, provides instructions, and makes product recommendations would benefit from instruction Fine-tuning.
- Choose classification Fine-tuning when the task involves strict categorization into predefined labels. A model designed to detect financial fraud by categorizing transactions as "fraudulent" or "non-fraudulent" would be a good candidate for classification Fine-tuning.

Recent developments in Fine-tuning techniques, such as parameter-efficient Fine-tuning methods like LoRA (Low-Rank Adaptation), Prompt Tuning, and Adapter Modules, have made it easier to adapt pre-trained models for specific tasks. These techniques require Fine-tuning only a subset of the model's parameters, significantly reducing computational requirements while maintaining performance. Both instruction and Classification Fine-Tuning play pivotal roles in tailoring language models for real-world applications. The choice of method depends on the nature of the task, resource availability, and the desired balance between versatility and precision. As AI research progresses, these Fine-tuning techniques are becoming more efficient, enabling broader accessibility and adaptability in deploying language models.

6.2 Preparing Data for Fine-tuning

To prepare for Fine-tuning a GPT-based model for text classification, we'll modify and use a dataset for training, validation, and testing. The following steps outline the process, with an updated example and detailed comments to make the code more comprehensible.

Downloading and Preparing the Dataset

The dataset contains messages labeled as "spam" or "not spam" (ham). We'll download, unzip, and prepare the dataset for use.

Updated Code Example:

```
import urllib.request
import zipfile
import os
from pathlib import Path

# Define the URL and paths for downloading and extracting the dataset
url = "https://archive.ics.uci.edu/ml/machine-learning-databases/00228/smsspamcollection.zip"
zip_path = "sms_spam_collection.zip"
extracted_path = "sms_spam_collection"
data_file_path = Path(extracted_path) / "SMSSpamCollection.tsv"

def download_and_unzip_spam_data(url, zip_path, extracted_path, data_file_path):
    """
    Downloads and unzips the spam dataset if it doesn't already exist locally.
    """
    if data_file_path.exists():
        print(f"{data_file_path} already exists. Skipping download and extraction.")
        return
```

```
    # Download the zip file
    with urllib.request.urlopen(url) as response:
        with open(zip_path, "wb") as out_file:
            out_file.write(response.read())

    # Extract the zip file
    with zipfile.ZipFile(zip_path, "r") as zip_ref:
        zip_ref.extractall(extracted_path)

    # Rename the extracted file to the desired path
    original_file_path = Path(extracted_path) / "SMSSpamCollection"
    os.rename(original_file_path, data_file_path)
    print(f"File downloaded and saved as {data_file_path}")

# Download and unzip the dataset
download_and_unzip_spam_data(url, zip_path, extracted_path, data_file_path)
```

Loading the Dataset

We'll load the downloaded data into a Pandas DataFrame for preprocessing.

```
import pandas as pd

# Load the dataset into a Pandas DataFrame
df = pd.read_csv(
    data_file_path, sep="\t", header=None, names=["Label", "Text"]
)

# Display the first few rows of the dataset
print(df.head())
```

Balancing the Dataset

Since the dataset is imbalanced (with more "ham" messages than "spam"), we'll balance it by undersampling the majority class.

```
def create_balanced_dataset(df):
    """
    Balances the dataset by undersampling the majority class.
    """
    num_spam = df[df["Label"] == "spam"].shape[0]  # Count spam instances
    ham_subset = df[df["Label"] == "ham"].sample(num_spam, random_state=123)  # Undersample ham
    balanced_df = pd.concat([ham_subset, df[df["Label"] == "spam"]])  # Combine the subsets
    return balanced_df

# Balance the dataset
balanced_df = create_balanced_dataset(df)
print(balanced_df["Label"].value_counts())
```

Encoding Class Labels

To prepare for training, we convert the string labels "ham" and "spam" into numerical labels: 0 for "ham" and 1 for "spam."

```
# Map class labels to numerical values
balanced_df["Label"] = balanced_df["Label"].map({"ham": 0, "spam": 1})

# Verify the mapping
print(balanced_df.head())
```

Splitting the Dataset

We split the dataset into training, validation, and testing subsets with a 70-10-20 ratio.

```
def random_split(df, train_frac, validation_frac):
    """
    Splits the dataset into training, validation, and testing subsets.
```

```
    """
    # Shuffle and reset the index
    df = df.sample(frac=1, random_state=123).reset_index(drop=True)
    train_end = int(len(df) * train_frac)
    validation_end = train_end + int(len(df) * validation_frac)

    # Create the splits
    train_df = df[:train_end]
    validation_df = df[train_end:validation_end]
    test_df = df[validation_end:]
    return train_df, validation_df, test_df

# Split the dataset
train_df, validation_df, test_df = random_split(balanced_df, 0.7, 0.1)

# Save the splits to CSV for reuse
train_df.to_csv("train.csv", index=False)
validation_df.to_csv("validation.csv", index=False)
test_df.to_csv("test.csv", index=False)

# Verify the splits
print(f"Training set: {len(train_df)} examples")
print(f"Validation set: {len(validation_df)} examples")
print(f"Testing set: {len(test_df)} examples")
```

Alternative Dataset Example

Instead of spam classification, consider a dataset for sentiment analysis. For instance, a dataset with product reviews labeled as "positive" or "negative." The steps to download, preprocess, and balance the data would remain similar.

```
url = "https://example.com/sentiment_dataset.zip"
zip_path = "sentiment_dataset.zip"
```

```
extracted_path = "sentiment_dataset"
data_file_path = Path(extracted_path) / "SentimentData.tsv"


# Follow similar steps for downloading and processing
# Labels can be mapped: "positive" -> 1, "negative" -> 0
```

With the dataset prepared, balanced, and split into subsets, we are now ready to set up data loaders for training a GPT-based model. This structured process ensures the model is trained effectively, handles class imbalances, and evaluates its performance reliably.

6.3 Building Data Loaders

To prepare for Fine-tuning a GPT-based model for text classification, we first set up PyTorch data loaders using a spam dataset. These data loaders will standardize and batch the input data for training, validation, and testing. The following steps outline the process, with updated examples, detailed explanations, and proper code comments.

Setting Up a Dataset Class

The dataset contains text messages of varying lengths. To train the model efficiently, we need to ensure all messages in a batch have the same length. This can be achieved by padding shorter messages to match the longest message's length. We'll use the token ID 50256 (<|endoftext|>) as the padding token.

Updated Code Example with Detailed Comments:

```
import torch
from torch.utils.data import Dataset
import pandas as pd


class SpamDataset(Dataset):
    """
    A custom PyTorch Dataset for loading and processing spam text messages.
    This dataset handles tokenization, padding, and truncation of text messages.
    """
    def __init__(self, csv_file, tokenizer, max_length=None, pad_token_id=50256):
        # Load the dataset from the CSV file
```

```
        self.data = pd.read_csv(csv_file)

        # Tokenize all text messages
        self.encoded_texts = [tokenizer.encode(text) for text in self.data["Text"]]

        # Determine the maximum sequence length (longest message) if not provided
        if max_length is None:
            self.max_length = self._longest_encoded_length()
        else:
            self.max_length = max_length

        # Truncate all sequences to the maximum length
        self.encoded_texts = [
            encoded_text[:self.max_length]
            for encoded_text in self.encoded_texts
        ]

        # Pad all sequences to the maximum length
        self.encoded_texts = [
            encoded_text + [pad_token_id] * (self.max_length - len(encoded_text))
            for encoded_text in self.encoded_texts
        ]

    def __getitem__(self, index):
        """
        Retrieve a single example (encoded text and its label) from the dataset.
        """

encoded = self.encoded_texts[index]
        label = self.data.iloc[index]["Label"]
```

```
        return (
            torch.tensor(encoded, dtype=torch.long),  # Input sequence
            torch.tensor(label, dtype=torch.long)     # Corresponding label
        )

    def __len__(self):
        """
        Return the total number of examples in the dataset.
        """
        return len(self.data)

    def _longest_encoded_length(self):
        """
        Compute the length of the longest encoded sequence in the dataset.
        """
        return max(len(encoded_text) for encoded_text in self.encoded_texts)

# Example usage of the dataset class
tokenizer = tiktoken.get_encoding("gpt2")
train_dataset = SpamDataset(csv_file="train.csv", tokenizer=tokenizer)
print(f"Longest sequence length: {train_dataset.max_length}")
```

Preparing Validation and Test Sets

To ensure consistent input sizes across datasets, we pad the validation and test sets to match the longest sequence in the training set.

```
val_dataset = SpamDataset(
    csv_file="validation.csv",
    tokenizer=tokenizer,
    max_length=train_dataset.max_length  # Match training set length
)
```

```
test_dataset = SpamDataset(
    csv_file="test.csv",
    tokenizer=tokenizer,
    max_length=train_dataset.max_length  # Match training set length
)
```

Setting Up Data Loaders

Data loaders provide an efficient way to load data in batches for training and evaluation.

```
from torch.utils.data import DataLoader
# Define data loader parameters
batch_size = 8
num_workers = 0  # Use a single worker for simplicity

# Create data loaders for training, validation, and testing
train_loader = DataLoader(
    dataset=train_dataset,
    batch_size=batch_size,
    shuffle=True,  # Shuffle data for training
    num_workers=num_workers,
    drop_last=True  # Drop incomplete batches
)

val_loader = DataLoader(
    dataset=val_dataset,
    batch_size=batch_size,
    shuffle=False,  # No need to shuffle validation data
    num_workers=num_workers
)

test_loader = DataLoader(
    dataset=test_dataset,
```

```
    batch_size=batch_size,
    shuffle=False,  # No need to shuffle test data
    num_workers=num_workers
)
```

Testing the Data Loaders

Verify that the data loaders return batches with the correct dimensions.

```
# Iterate through the training loader to confirm dimensions
for input_batch, target_batch in train_loader:
    pass  # Process each batch (omitted for demonstration)

# Print dimensions of a sample batch
print("Input batch dimensions:", input_batch.shape)
print("Label batch dimensions:", target_batch.shape)
```

Alternative Example: Sentiment Analysis Dataset

Instead of spam classification, consider a sentiment analysis dataset where text messages are labeled as "positive" (1) or "negative" (0). Adjust the dataset and labels accordingly.

Sample Dataset Preparation:

```
sentiment_data = {
    "Text": ["I love this product!", "Worst experience ever.", "Absolutely fantastic!", "Not
      worth the price."],
    "Label": [1, 0, 1, 0]
}

# Save the dataset as a CSV file
sentiment_df = pd.DataFrame(sentiment_data)
sentiment_df.to_csv("sentiment.csv", index=False)

Update Dataset Class:
sentiment_dataset = SpamDataset(
```

```
    csv_file="sentiment.csv",
    tokenizer=tokenizer,
    max_length=None  # Automatically adjust to the longest sequence
)
```

Batch Summary

Finally, calculate and display the number of batches for each dataset.

```
print(f"{len(train_loader)} training batches")
print(f"{len(val_loader)} validation batches")
print(f"{len(test_loader)} test batches")
```

With the dataset prepared and the data loaders tested, we are now ready to move forward with model Fine-tuning. These data loaders ensure efficient training by batching input data and labels while handling sequence length variability with padding. This process is extensible to various text-based classification tasks, such as sentiment analysis, topic categorisation, or intent detection.

6.4 Initializing a Model with Existing Pretrained Weights

To prepare a pretrained GPT model for classification Fine-tuning to identify spam messages, we must initialize the model with the appropriate configurations, load its pretrained weights, and evaluate its readiness for Fine-tuning. The following steps demonstrate the process with detailed explanations and updated code.

Step 1: Define Model Configuration

We begin by selecting the GPT model variant (e.g., gpt2-small) and setting up its base configuration. This includes parameters such as vocabulary size, context length, dropout rate, and attention mechanisms. Additionally, we specify model-specific configurations such as embedding dimensions, the number of layers, and the number of attention heads.

Updated Code Example with Comments:

```
# Define the model size and input prompt for testing
CHOOSE_MODEL = "gpt2-small (124M)"
INPUT_PROMPT = "Every effort moves"

# Base configuration for the GPT model
```

```
BASE_CONFIG = {
    "vocab_size": 50257,        # Vocabulary size
    "context_length": 1024,     # Maximum sequence length
    "drop_rate": 0.0,           # Dropout rate
    "qkv_bias": True            # Bias in attention mechanisms
}

# Model-specific configurations
model_configs = {
    "gpt2-small (124M)": {"emb_dim": 768, "n_layers": 12, "n_heads": 12},
    "gpt2-medium (355M)": {"emb_dim": 1024, "n_layers": 24, "n_heads": 16},
    "gpt2-large (774M)": {"emb_dim": 1280, "n_layers": 36, "n_heads": 20},
    "gpt2-xl (1558M)": {"emb_dim": 1600, "n_layers": 48, "n_heads": 25},
}

# Update the base configuration with the selected model's settings
BASE_CONFIG.update(model_configs[CHOOSE_MODEL])
```

Step 2: Load Pretrained Weights

To initialize the model, we load pretrained weights using a utility function. This ensures the model has been pretrained on extensive datasets and can serve as a solid foundation for classification Fine-tuning.

```
from gpt_download import download_and_load_gpt2
from chapter05 import GPTModel, load_weights_into_gpt

# Extract model size from the chosen model name
model_size = CHOOSE_MODEL.split(" ")[-1].lstrip("(").rstrip(")")

# Download and load the pretrained model weights
settings, params = download_and_load_gpt2(
    model_size=model_size, models_dir="gpt2"
```

```
)
# Initialize the GPT model with the chosen configuration
model = GPTModel(BASE_CONFIG)

# Load the pretrained weights into the model
load_weights_into_gpt(model, params)

# Set the model to evaluation mode
model.eval()
```

Step 3: Test the Pretrained Model

Before Fine-tuning, we validate that the model has been initialized correctly by generating text based on a simple input prompt.

```
import generate_text_simple
import text_to_token_ids, token_ids_to_text


# Define a test input prompt
text_1 = "Every effort moves you"
# Generate text using the pretrained model
token_ids = generate_text_simple(
    model=model,
    idx=text_to_token_ids(text_1, tokenizer),
    max_new_tokens=15,  # Limit the number of new tokens to generate
    context_size=BASE_CONFIG["context_length"]
)
# Decode and print the generated text
print(token_ids_to_text(token_ids, tokenizer))
```

Expected Output:

Every effort moves you forward.

The first step is to understand the importance of your work.

This confirms that the model weights have been correctly loaded and the model can generate coherent text.

Step 4: Evaluate Classification Capability

Next, we check whether the model can already classify spam messages by providing it with a prompt and evaluating its response.

```
# Define a classification prompt for the pretrained model
text_2 = (
    "Is the following text 'spam'? Answer with 'yes' or 'no':"
    " 'You are a winner you have been specially"
    " selected to receive $1000 cash or a $2000 award.'"
)

# Generate a response to the classification prompt
token_ids = generate_text_simple(
    model=model,
    idx=text_to_token_ids(text_2, tokenizer),
    max_new_tokens=23,
    context_size=BASE_CONFIG["context_length"]
)

# Decode and print the model's response
print(token_ids_to_text(token_ids, tokenizer))
```

Expected Output:

Is the following text 'spam'? Answer with 'yes' or 'no': 'You are a winner

you have been specially selected to receive 100000 cash or a 200000 award.'

The following text 'spam'? Answer with 'yes' or 'no': 'You are a winner

This output suggests the model struggles to follow the classification instructions. This is expected, as the model has only undergone unsupervised Pretraining and lacks Fine-tuning for instruction-following or classification tasks.

Step 5: Prepare for Classification Fine-tuning

To fine-tune the model for spam classification, we will:

1. Modify its architecture (if needed) to include a classification head.
2. Fine-tune it on a labelled spam dataset using supervised learning.

The Fine-tuning process will involve:

- Feeding labelled data (spam and not spam) into the model.
- Optimizing the model to minimise the classification error.
- Using the trained model to classify unseen text messages accurately.

The steps above ensure that the pretrained GPT model is initialized correctly and ready for Fine-tuning. While the model performs well for text generation, it lacks the specific capabilities required for spam classification. By applying classification Fine-tuning, the model can be trained to understand and categorize text based on the labelled data, enabling it to identify spam messages effectively.

6.5 Attaching a Classification Head

To prepare a pretrained language model (LLM) for classification Fine-tuning, we adapt its architecture by replacing the output layer to map the hidden representation to binary class labels. Additionally, we selectively configure certain layers for training while freezing others, ensuring the model is optimized for its new classification task (e.g., identifying "spam" and "not spam"). Below are the model modifications steps, with detailed explanations and code examples.

Step 1: Review the Model Architecture

Before modifications, we inspect the model's architecture to understand its structure and identify the layer to be replaced.

```
# Print the model architecture to understand its structure
print(model)

# Example output shows layers such as embeddings, transformer blocks, LayerNorm,
    and the output head:

# (out_head): Linear(in_features=768, out_features=50257, bias=False)
```

The out_head layer is the original output layer, mapping the hidden representation to a vocabulary size of 50,257. For classification, this layer will be replaced.

Step 2: Freeze Non-Trainable Layers

To fine-tune efficiently, we freeze all parameters in the model to make them non-trainable, ensuring only the relevant layers are updated.

```
# Freeze all model parameters
for param in model.parameters():
    param.requires_grad = False
```

Step 3: Replace the Output Layer

We replace the original output layer (out_head) with a new layer that maps the hidden representation to two classes: 0 (not spam) and 1 (spam).

```
import torch
# Set random seed for reproducibility
torch.manual_seed(123)

# Define the number of output classes
num_classes = 2

# Replace the output layer with a binary classification head
model.out_head = torch.nn.Linear(
    in_features=BASE_CONFIG["emb_dim"],  # Match embedding dimension
    out_features=num_classes             # Two classes for binary classification
)
```

The requires_grad attribute of the new output layer is True by default, making it trainable during Fine-tuning.

Step 4: Fine-Tune Additional Layers

In addition to the output layer, Fine-tuning the last transformer block and the final normalization layer can significantly improve model performance.

```
# Make the last transformer block trainable
for param in model.trf_blocks[-1].parameters():
    param.requires_grad = True
```

```
# Make the final LayerNorm trainable
for param in model.final_norm.parameters():
    param.requires_grad = True
```

This approach balances computational efficiency with improved Fine-tuning results.

Step 5: Test the Modified Model

To verify the model's modifications, pass a sample input through the model and inspect its outputs.

```
# Encode a sample input text
inputs = tokenizer.encode("Is this spam?")
inputs = torch.tensor(inputs).unsqueeze(0)  # Add batch dimension

# Print input details
print("Inputs:", inputs)
print("Inputs dimensions:", inputs.shape)

# Pass the input through the model
with torch.no_grad():
    outputs = model(inputs)


# Print the model outputs
print("Outputs:\n", outputs)
print("Outputs dimensions:", outputs.shape)
```

Sample Output:

```
Inputs: tensor([[5021, 572, 319, 2335]])
Inputs dimensions: torch.Size([1, 4])
Outputs:
 tensor([[[-1.2345, 0.7654],
         [-2.4567, 1.9876],
         [-1.6789, 2.3456],
         [-0.5678, 1.1234]]])
Outputs dimensions: torch.Size([1, 4, 2])
```

The dimensions indicate:

- Batch size: 1 (the number of examples in the input batch).
- Sequence length: 4 (the number of input tokens).
- Output size: 2 (corresponding to the two classes).

Step 6: Focus on the Last Token

In GPT-like models, the last token's output accumulates the most information due to the causal attention mechanism. For classification, we focus on the last token.

```
# Extract the output corresponding to the last token
last_output = outputs[:, -1, :]
print("Last output token:", last_output)
```

```
Sample Output:
Last output token: tensor([[-0.5678, 1.1234]])
```

Step 7: Transform Outputs to Class Predictions

To convert the model's outputs into class predictions, apply a softmax function followed by a prediction step.

```
import torch.nn.functional as F

# Apply softmax to transform logits into probabilities
probabilities = F.softmax(last_output, dim=-1)
print("Class probabilities:", probabilities)


# Get the predicted class
predicted_class = torch.argmax(probabilities, dim=-1)
print("Predicted class:", predicted_class)
```

Sample Output:

```
Class probabilities: tensor([[0.3123, 0.6877]])
Predicted class: tensor([1])
```

The model predicts the input as class 1 (spam).

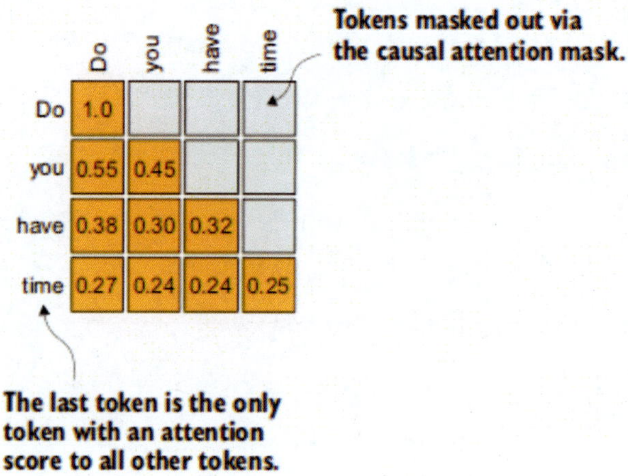

The modified model now includes a classification head tailored for binary classification tasks. We ensure the model is prepared for efficient and effective classification Fine-tuning by Fine-tuning the output layer and selectively adjusting additional layers. This approach can be adapted to various tasks, including sentiment analysis, topic classification, and more.

6.6 Calculating Loss and Accuracy for Classification

To prepare a pretrained language model for Fine-tuning on a classification task, we need to implement evaluation functions to assess its performance before and during Fine-tuning. This involves calculating the model's classification accuracy and loss. Here, we outline the process, provide updated examples, and include comprehensive comments.

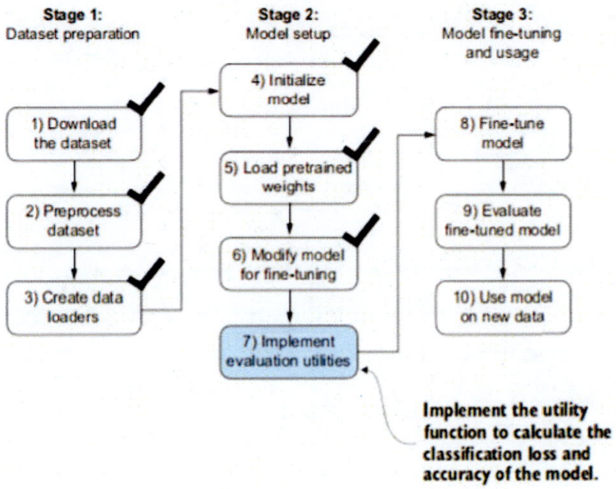

The three-stage process for classification Fine-tuning of the LLM involves multiple steps. Having completed the first six steps, we are now ready to finalize stage 2 by implementing the functions required to evaluate the model's performance in classifying spam messages before, during, and after the Fine-tuning process.

Step 1: Predicting Class Labels

To predict whether the input text is "spam" or "not spam," we use the logits output for the last token in the sequence. The class label is determined by the index of the maximum value in the logits.

Code Example:

```
import torch

# Assume `outputs` is the model's output tensor for an input batch
# For demonstration, we use a dummy tensor representing the logits for the last token
outputs = torch.tensor([[[-3.5983, 3.9902]]]) # Shape: [1, 1, 2]

# Extract the logits for the last token
logits = outputs[:, -1, :] # Shape: [batch_size, num_classes]
```

```
# Predict the class label using argmax
predicted_label = torch.argmax(logits, dim=-1)  # Shape: [batch_size]
print("Class label:", predicted_label.item())
```

Output:

```
Class label: 1
```

Step 2: Calculating Classification Accuracy

Classification accuracy measures the percentage of correct predictions across a dataset. We iterate over the data loader, predict labels for each batch, and compare them with the true labels.

Code Example:

```
def calc_accuracy_loader(data_loader, model, device, num_batches=None):
    """
    Calculate classification accuracy for a given data loader.
    Parameters:
        data_loader (DataLoader): PyTorch DataLoader for the dataset.
        model (torch.nn.Module): Pretrained model to evaluate.
        device (torch.device): Device (CPU or GPU) for computation.
          num_batches (int, optional): Number of batches to evaluate. If None, use all
        batches.
    Returns:
        float: Accuracy as a percentage of correct predictions.
    """
    model.eval()  # Set the model to evaluation mode
    correct_predictions, num_examples = 0, 0

    # Determine the number of batches to evaluate
    num_batches = num_batches or len(data_loader)
    for i, (input_batch, target_batch) in enumerate(data_loader):
        if i >= num_batches:
            break
```

```
        # Move data to the specified device
        input_batch = input_batch.to(device)
        target_batch = target_batch.to(device)

        with torch.no_grad():  # Disable gradient computation for evaluation
            logits = model(input_batch)[:, -1, :] # Get logits for the last token
            predicted_labels = torch.argmax(logits, dim=-1)  # Predict class labels

        # Update the counts
        num_examples += target_batch.size(0)
        correct_predictions += (predicted_labels == target_batch).sum().item()

    return correct_predictions / num_examples  # Return accuracy as a fraction
```

Step 3: Computing Loss

To train the model effectively, we calculate the cross-entropy loss, which measures the difference between the predicted probabilities and the true class labels. This loss guides the optimization process during training.

Code Example:

```
def calc_loss_batch(input_batch, target_batch, model, device):
    """
    Calculate the loss for a single batch.

Parameters:
        input_batch (torch.Tensor): Input batch of token IDs.
        target_batch (torch.Tensor): True labels for the batch.
        model (torch.nn.Module): Pretrained model.
        device (torch.device): Device (CPU or GPU) for computation.

Returns:
        torch.Tensor: The calculated loss.
    """
```

```
    # Move data to the specified device
    input_batch = input_batch.to(device)
    target_batch = target_batch.to(device)

    # Get the logits for the last token
    logits = model(input_batch)[:, -1, :]  # Shape: [batch_size, num_classes]

    # Calculate cross-entropy loss
    loss = torch.nn.functional.cross_entropy(logits, target_batch)
    return loss
```

To compute the loss across an entire dataset:

python

Copy code

```
def calc_loss_loader(data_loader, model, device, num_batches=None):
    """
    Calculate the average loss for a data loader.

    Parameters:
        data_loader (DataLoader): PyTorch DataLoader for the dataset.
        model (torch.nn.Module): Pretrained model to evaluate.
        device (torch.device): Device (CPU or GPU) for computation.
        num_batches (int, optional): Number of batches to evaluate. If None, use all batches.

    Returns:
        float: Average loss over the evaluated batches.
    """
    model.eval()  # Set the model to evaluation mode
    total_loss = 0.0
    # Determine the number of batches to evaluate
    num_batches = num_batches or len(data_loader)
```

```
    for i, (input_batch, target_batch) in enumerate(data_loader):
        if i >= num_batches:
            break

        # Calculate loss for the current batch
        loss = calc_loss_batch(input_batch, target_batch, model, device)
        total_loss += loss.item()

    return total_loss / num_batches  # Return average loss
```

Step 4: Evaluate the Model

Using the above utility functions, we can calculate the initial accuracy and loss across training, validation, and test datasets.

Code Example:

```
# Set device to GPU if available, otherwise CPU
device = torch.device("cuda" if torch.cuda.is_available() else "cpu")
model.to(device)  # Move the model to the device

# Calculate accuracy
train_accuracy=calc_accuracy_loader(train_loader, model, device, num_batches=10)
val_accuracy = calc_accuracy_loader(val_loader, model, device, num_batches=10)
test_accuracy = calc_accuracy_loader(test_loader, model, device, num_batches=10)

print(f"Training accuracy: {train_accuracy*100:.2f}%")
print(f"Validation accuracy: {val_accuracy*100:.2f}%")
print(f"Test accuracy: {test_accuracy*100:.2f}%")

# Calculate loss
with torch.no_grad():  # Disable gradient computation
    train_loss = calc_loss_loader(train_loader, model, device, num_batches=5)
    val_loss = calc_loss_loader(val_loader, model, device, num_batches=5)
```

```
    test_loss = calc_loss_loader(test_loader, model, device, num_batches=5)
print(f"Training loss: {train_loss:.3f}")
print(f"Validation loss: {val_loss:.3f}")
print(f"Test loss: {test_loss:.3f}")
```

Step 5: Example Use Case - Sentiment Analysis

The process remains the same for sentiment analysis, except the labels represent sentiments like "positive" (1) and "negative" (0).

Example:

```
# Predict sentiment
sample_input = tokenizer.encode("I love this product!")
sample_input = torch.tensor(sample_input).unsqueeze(0).to(device)
with torch.no_grad():
    logits = model(sample_input)[:, -1, :]
    predicted_sentiment = torch.argmax(logits, dim=-1)
        print("Predicted sentiment:", "Positive" if predicted_sentiment.item() == 1 else
        "Negative")
```

These evaluation functions calculate classification accuracy and loss, critical for assessing model performance during Fine-tuning. By employing this approach, we can systematically refine the model to improve its prediction accuracy for tasks like spam detection or sentiment analysis.

6.7 Applying the LLM for Spam Detection

Having fine-tuned and evaluated the model, it is now ready to classify text messages as "spam" or "not spam." We implement a classify_review function to process the input text, convert it into token IDs, and predict the corresponding class label using the fine-tuned model. This function can classify any given text after following preprocessing steps similar to those in the SpamDataset class.

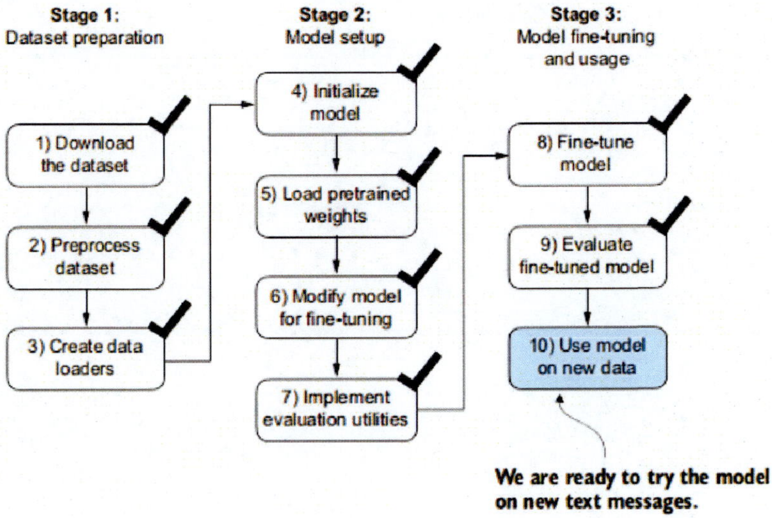

Additionally, we save the fine-tuned model to avoid retraining and reload it later for inference. Below is an updated and elaborated implementation.

Step 1: Define the classify_review Function

The function pre-processes input text, tokenizes it, pads or truncates it to the appropriate length, and uses the fine-tuned model to predict the class label.

Code Implementation:

```
def classify_review(text, model, tokenizer, device, max_length=None, pad_token_
    id=50256):
  """

  Classifies a given text as "spam" or "not spam" using the fine-tuned model.


  Parameters:
    text (str): The input text to classify.
    model (torch.nn.Module): The fine-tuned GPT-based classification model.
    tokenizer: Tokenizer for converting text to token IDs.
    device (torch.device): Device to run the model on (CPU or GPU).
    max_length (int, optional): Maximum sequence length for padding/truncation.
    pad_token_id (int, optional): Token ID for padding shorter sequences.
```

```
    Returns:
    str: The predicted class ("spam" or "not spam").
  """
  model.eval()  # Set the model to evaluation mode

  # Tokenize the input text and truncate if necessary
  input_ids = tokenizer.encode(text)
   supported_context_length = model.pos_emb.weight.shape[1]  # Maximum context
    length
  input_ids = input_ids[:min(max_length, supported_context_length)]
  # Pad the sequence to the required length
  input_ids += [pad_token_id] * (max_length - len(input_ids))

  # Convert input IDs to a tensor and add a batch dimension
  input_tensor = torch.tensor(input_ids, device=device).unsqueeze(0)

  # Get the model predictions
  with torch.no_grad():
    logits = model(input_tensor)[:, -1, :] # Extract logits for the last token
    predicted_label = torch.argmax(logits, dim=-1).item()  # Get the predicted class
  # Map the predicted label to a class name
  return "spam" if predicted_label == 1 else "not spam"
```

Step 2: Test the classify_review Function

We test the function with various text examples, ensuring it predicts the correct labels.

Code Example:

```
# Example 1: Spam message
text_1 = (
  "Congratulations! You've been selected to receive a $500 gift card."
  " Click the link below to claim your prize now."
)
```

```
result_1 = classify_review(text_1, model, tokenizer, device,
max_length=train_dataset.max_length)
print(f"Text: {text_1}\nPrediction: {result_1}\n")

# Example 2: Non-spam message
text_2 = (
    "Hi there, just confirming our meeting tomorrow at 3 PM."
    " Let me know if anything changes!"
)
result_2 = classify_review(text_2, model, tokenizer, device,
max_length=train_dataset.max_length)
print(f"Text: {text_2}\nPrediction: {result_2}\n")

# Example 3: Ambiguous message
text_3 = (
    "Limited-time offer! Buy one, get one free. Visit our store today!"
)
result_3 = classify_review(text_3, model, tokenizer, device,
max_length=train_dataset.max_length)
print(f"Text: {text_3}\nPrediction: {result_3}\n")
```

Step 3: Save the Fine-Tuned Model

To avoid retraining the model, save its state to a file.

Code Example:

```
# Save the fine-tuned model's state
torch.save(model.state_dict(), "spam_classifier.pth")
print("Model saved successfully.")
```

Step 4: Load the Saved Model

Reload the saved model for inference without retraining.

Code Example:

```
# Load the saved model state
model_state_dict = torch.load("spam_classifier.pth", map_location=device)
model.load_state_dict(model_state_dict)
model.eval()  # Ensure the model is in evaluation mode
print("Model loaded successfully.")
```

Step 5: Alternative Use Case - Sentiment Analysis

We can adapt the same function to perform sentiment analysis (e.g., classify text as "positive" or "negative") by changing the labels.

Example:

```
# Example for sentiment analysis
text = "I absolutely love this product! It works like a charm."
result = classify_review(text, model, tokenizer, device, max_length=train_dataset.max_
    length)
print(f"Text: {text}\nSentiment: {'Positive' if result == 'not spam' else 'Negative'}")
```

The classify_review function allows for efficient text classification using the fine-tuned model. It handles tokenization, padding, and inference seamlessly. Additionally, saving and reloading the model ensures reproducibility and avoids retraining, making it versatile for various classification tasks.

SUMMARY

- ✓ The chapter begins by detailing building a Large Language Model (LLM), Pretraining it on extensive datasets, and exploring methods to import pretrained weights from external sources, enabling a strong foundational understanding for Fine-tuning.
- ✓ Fine-tuning is a critical step to adapt LLMs for specific tasks like text classification or instruction-following, with examples ranging from spam detection to sentiment analysis, emphasizing the importance of task-specific datasets and efficient training methods.

✓ Two primary Fine-tuning approaches are discussed: Classification Fine-Tuning for precise categorization into predefined labels and Instruction Fine-Tuning for enabling LLMs to handle diverse user instructions. Both methods cater to different objectives, balancing versatility and specificity.

✓ The chapter introduces techniques like parameter-efficient Fine-tuning (e.g., LoRA, adapter modules) to enhance computational efficiency, allowing Fine-tuning on selected layers while preserving the core capabilities of the pretrained model.

✓ A comprehensive explanation is provided for preparing datasets, including downloading, balancing, splitting into subsets, and setting up PyTorch data loaders, ensuring efficient input processing for classification tasks.

✓ The final sections cover evaluating the model's performance using functions to calculate accuracy and loss, implementing classification utilities for tasks like spam detection, and saving/reloading the fine-tuned model to avoid retraining, ensuring reproducibility and versatility for other tasks like sentiment analysis.

Exercises

Exercise 1 – Multiple Choice Questions

1. Which of the following methods reduces computational resources required for Fine-tuning Large Language Models ?

    a) Gradient Descent

    b) Parameter-Efficient Fine-tuning (e.g., LoRA)

    c) Data Augmentation

    d) Softmax Scaling

2. What is the primary goal of classification Fine-tuning?

    a) To generate text-based responses

    b) To handle diverse tasks with instructions

    c) To categorize data into specific predefined labels

    d) To improve model vocabulary

Exercise 2 – One Word Answers

1. What token is used to pad sequences in GPT-based models?
2. Which function converts logits into probabilities in classification tasks?

Exercise 3 – Short Answers

1. Why is padding used when preparing datasets for Fine-tuning?
2. What is the significance of the last token in GPT-based classification tasks?

Exercise 4 – Long Answers

1. Explain the differences between Instruction Fine-Tuning and Classification Fine-Tuning in language models.
2. Describe the process of preparing a dataset for Fine-Tuning an LLM

Answers

Exercise 1- 1) b, 2) c

Exercise 2- 1) <|endoftext|>, 2) Softmax

Online Resources

	Practice Paper	YouTube Video Playlist Link
Link	https://forms.gle/PEGRFw6rYJ2kivPc9	https://www.youtube.com/playlist?list=PLzlh_31VWEFoDAL0w66iI-aLkpQ9E-Wcw
QR Code		

Chapter

7

FINE-TUNING TO FOLLOW INSTRUCTIONS

In this chapter you will learn about:

- ☐ Basics of Instruction Fine-Tuning
- ☐ Dataset for Instruction Fine-Tuning
- ☐ Structuring Data into Batches for Training
- ☐ Setting Up Data Loaders for Instruction-Based Datasets
- ☐ Loading a Pretrained Language Model
- ☐ Training the LLM on Instructional Data
- ☐ Extracting and Saving Output Responses

Previously, we developed a Large Language Model (LLM) architecture, conducted Pretraining on vast datasets, and successfully integrated pretrained weights sourced externally. This foundational work laid the groundwork for customizing the LLM for specific tasks. One of the key tasks we explored was Fine-tuning the model for classification purposes, such as identifying and categorising text messages as spam or non-spam. This Fine-tuning process demonstrated how pretrained models could be adapted for high-accuracy performance in targeted scenarios.

Now, the focus shifts toward an advanced Fine-tuning technique that enables LLMs to understand better and respond to human instructions. Instruction Fine-Tuning is pivotal for applications like chatbots, virtual personal assistants, and other conversational AI systems where natural, context-aware interaction is essential.

The process of Instruction Fine-Tuning involves training the model on a curated dataset specifically designed to teach the LLM how to follow diverse human prompts effectively. These datasets often include examples of various instructions paired with the expected model responses, enabling the LLM to generalize across a wide range of conversational tasks.

Example Scenarios for Instruction Fine-tuning

1. **Customer Support:** Fine-tuning a model to assist with customer queries in e-commerce. For instance, given an instruction like "Help me find a pair of running shoes under Rs.50," the model learns to provide specific product suggestions based on the instruction.

2. **Educational Assistance:** Training the LLM to act as a tutor. With prompts like "Explain photosynthesis to a 7th class student," the model can adapt its response to the appropriate level of detail and complexity.

3. **Creative Writing Support:** Fine-tuning the model to aid writers. Instructions such as "Write a poem about the ocean in a nostalgic tone" help the model produce creative content aligned with specific styles and emotions.

4. **Programming Help:** Enabling the model to assist developers by understanding technical instructions. For example, a prompt like "Write a Python function to calculate the Fibonacci sequence" would result in accurate and efficient code generation.

5. **Personal Productivity:** Training the LLM for task management, such as responding to "Create a daily schedule for me that includes 30 minutes of exercise, 1 hour of reading, and 8 hours of work."

The process involves selecting high-quality instruction-response pairs that cover diverse domains and contexts. The model's ability to generalize improves with exposure to instructions that vary in complexity, specificity, and structure. This Fine-tuning method not only enhances the usability of LLMs but also opens up avenues for creating highly versatile AI systems tailored for both professional and personal use. By focusing on instruction-following capabilities, the model can evolve from being a static knowledge repository to a dynamic tool that interacts meaningfully with users in real-world scenarios

7.1 Basics of Instruction Fine-tuning

Pretraining a Large Language Model (LLM) involves a training process where the model learns to predict the next word in a sequence based on the context provided by the preceding words. This task, often referred to as causal language modelling, enables the LLM to develop a deep understanding of linguistic patterns, grammar, and contextual relationships. The result is a pretrained LLM capable of text generation tasks such as completing sentences or creating paragraphs from a given text fragment. For example, if provided with the input "The sun rises in the east, and...", then the model might predict a continuation like "sets in the west."

While such pretrained models are adept at generic text generation, they often struggle with tasks that require following specific instructions. For instance, requests like "Fix the grammar in this text" or "Rewrite this sentence in the passive voice" demand a level of understanding and precision that goes beyond simple text prediction. This is where instruction Fine-tuning becomes essential. By refining the model's ability to follow detailed instructions, we can significantly enhance its utility in various applications.

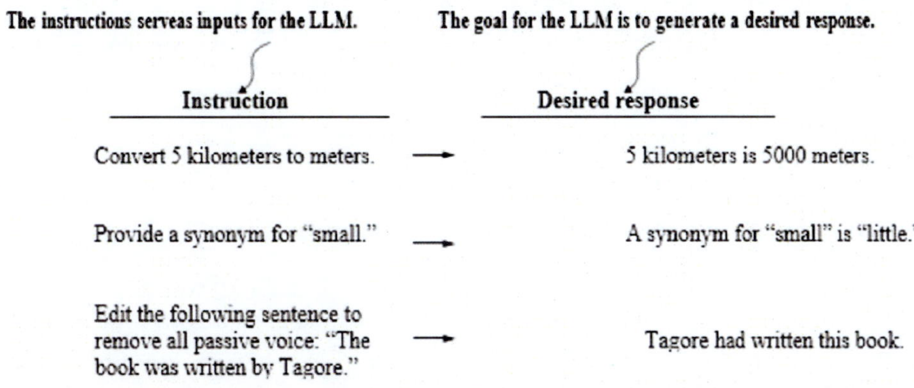

These examples demonstrate how LLMs process specific instructions to produce tailored and contextually appropriate outputs.

The Process of Instruction Fine-tuning

Instruction Fine-Tuning involves training the model on datasets designed to improve its understanding of and responsiveness to specific instructions. This process enables the model to adapt to user-defined tasks and generate outputs aligned with the desired outcomes. Fine-tuning involves three main stages:

1. Dataset Preparation: The foundation of instruction Fine-tuning lies in high-quality datasets. These datasets consist of input-output pairs where the input specifies the instruction, and the output provides the expected response. Examples include:

- o Input: "Correct the grammar of this sentence: 'He go to school yesterday.'" Output: "He went to school yesterday."
- o Input: "Summarize this paragraph in one sentence: [paragraph text]" Output: "[Summarized sentence]"

  To maximize the model's versatility, datasets often cover diverse instructions across multiple domains, such as grammar correction, style transformation, summarization, and question answering.

2. Model Training: Using the curated dataset, the LLM undergoes supervised Fine-tuning. This involves training the model to minimize the discrepancy between its predicted outputs and the expected responses in the dataset. Techniques such as cross-entropy loss are typically employed to optimize the model's performance.
3. Evaluation and Iteration: After Fine-tuning, the model's performance is evaluated against a validation dataset. Metrics like BLEU, ROUGE, or task-specific accuracy scores are used to assess how well the model adheres to instructions. Based on the evaluation, additional adjustments to the dataset or Fine-tuning process may be made to further enhance performance.

By enhancing the ability of LLMs to follow instructions, Fine-tuning transforms them into versatile tools capable of addressing a wide range of practical tasks. This process bridges the gap between general-purpose pretrained models and task-specific AI systems, unlocking their potential for more precise and user-centric applications.

7.2 Preparing a Supervised Dataset for Instruction Fine-tuning

To fine-tune a pretrained Large Language Model (LLM) for instruction-following tasks, we start by downloading, processing, and preparing a dataset of instruction-response pairs. This dataset provides a foundation for teaching the model to understand and respond effectively to specific instructions. Here, we demonstrate how to structure this process, including downloading the dataset, formatting it into a usable style for training, and partitioning it into training, validation, and test sets.

Pretrained LLMs, while proficient at generating text, often struggle to perform tasks that require interpreting precise instructions. Fine-tuning with instruction datasets bridges this gap, enabling models to deliver responses tailored to user queries, such as grammar correction, text transformation, and semantic reasoning.

Step 1: Downloading and Loading the Dataset

The dataset contains 1,100 instruction-response pairs stored in a JSON file. The following function downloads the file if it doesn't exist locally and loads the data:

```
import json
import os
import urllib

def download_and_load_file(file_path, url):
    """
    Download a JSON file from the specified URL if it doesn't exist locally,
    and load its contents into a Python object.

    Args:
        file_path (str): Local file path to save the dataset.
        url (str): URL to download the dataset from.

    Returns:
        data (list): Parsed JSON data as a Python list of dictionaries.
    """
    # Check if file already exists locally
    if not os.path.exists(file_path):
        # Download the file from the URL
        with urllib.request.urlopen(url) as response:
            text_data = response.read().decode("utf-8")
        # Save the downloaded file locally
        with open(file_path, "w", encoding="utf-8") as file:
            file.write(text_data)
    # Load the file contents into a Python object
    with open(file_path, "r", encoding="utf-8") as file:
        data = json.load(file)
    return data

# File path and URL of the dataset
file_path = "instruction-data.json"
```

```
url = (
    "https://raw.githubusercontent.com/rasbt/LLMs-from-scratch"
    "/main/ch07/01_main-chapter-code/instruction-data.json"
)

# Load the dataset
data = download_and_load_file(file_path, url)
print("Number of entries:", len(data))
```

Output:

```
Number of entries: 1100
```

Step 2: Inspecting and Formatting Dataset Entries

Each dataset entry is a dictionary with instruction, input, and output fields. We define a function to format these entries for Fine-tuning in an LLM-friendly style.

```
def format_input(entry):
    """
    Format a dataset entry into a structured text format suitable for Fine-tuning.

    Args:
        entry (dict): A single entry containing 'instruction', 'input', and 'output'.

    Returns:
        str: Formatted input string.
    """
    # Base instruction text
    instruction_text = (
        "Below is an instruction that describes a task. "
        "Write a response that appropriately completes the request."
        f"\n\n### Instruction:\n{entry['instruction']}"
    )
```

```
# Include input text if available
input_text = f"\n\n### Input:\n{entry['input']}" if entry["input"] else ""
return instruction_text + input_text
```

Example Entries:

1. With Input:

```
model_input = format_input(data[50])
desired_response = f"\n\n### Response:\n{data[50]['output']}"
print(model_input + desired_response)
```

Output:

Below is an instruction that describes a task. Write a response that appropriately completes the request.

Instruction:

Identify the correct spelling of the following word.

Input:

Ocassion

Response:

The correct spelling is 'Occasion.'

2. Without Input:

```
model_input = format_input(data[999])
desired_response = f"\n\n### Response:\n{data[999]['output']}"
print(model_input + desired_response)
```

Output:

Below is an instruction that describes a task. Write a response that appropriately completes the request.

Instruction:

What is an antonym of 'complicated'?

Response:

An antonym of 'complicated' is 'simple.'

Step 3: Splitting the Dataset

We divide the dataset into training, validation, and test sets to evaluate and fine-tune the model effectively.

```
# Define split proportions
train_portion = int(len(data) * 0.85)  # 85% for training
test_portion = int(len(data) * 0.1)    # 10% for testing
val_portion = len(data) - train_portion - test_portion  # Remainder for validation

# Split the dataset
train_data = data[:train_portion]
test_data = data[train_portion:train_portion + test_portion]
val_data = data[train_portion + test_portion:]

# Display dataset sizes
print("Training set length:", len(train_data))
print("Validation set length:", len(val_data))
print("Test set length:", len(test_data))
```

Output:

```
Training set length: 935
Validation set length: 55
Test set length: 110
```

Key Updates:

1. Increased Dataset Examples: Publicly available datasets such as OpenAI's prompt datasets or Microsoft's TaskOrientedDialog can be explored for extended instruction Fine-tuning.
2. Enhanced Model Performance: Techniques like instruction tuning with reinforcement learning from human feedback (RLHF) can further refine LLM responses.

3. Real-World Applications: Fine-tuned LLMs can improve the accuracy of tasks like legal document summarization, sentiment analysis, or technical writing.

This structured approach ensures the dataset is ready for Fine-tuning, preparing the LLM to handle instruction-following tasks effectively.

7.3 Structuring Data into Batches for Training

Instruction Fine-Tuning involves enhancing a pretrained Large Language Model (LLM) to follow specific instructions effectively. This process requires thoughtful implementation of batching strategies to ensure efficient and precise model training. This document explains how to construct custom data batches for Instruction Fine-Tuning, implement padding, and manage token masking for optimal training outcomes.

Custom Dataset and Tokenization Class

The first step involves defining a dataset class, Instruction Dataset, to handle input formatting and tokenization. This class prepares the dataset by tokenizing the input-output pairs and storing them for efficient access during training.

```
import torch
from torch.utils.data import Dataset

class InstructionDataset(Dataset):
    """
    A custom dataset class for handling instruction Fine-tuning datasets.

    Args:
        data (list): A list of dictionaries with 'instruction', 'input', and 'output'.
        tokenizer: A tokenizer object to encode text inputs and outputs.
    """
    def __init__(self, data, tokenizer):
        self.data = data
        self.encoded_texts = []
        for entry in data:
            # Format the input using a pre-defined function
            instruction_plus_input = format_input(entry)
```

```
            response_text = f"\n\n### Response:\n{entry['output']}"
            full_text = instruction_plus_input + response_text
            # Tokenize and store the encoded text
            self.encoded_texts.append(tokenizer.encode(full_text))

    def __getitem__(self, index):
        """Returns the tokenized data for a given index."""
        return self.encoded_texts[index]

    def __len__(self):
        """Returns the total number of data samples."""
        return len(self.data)
```

Padding and Batch Construction

In Fine-tuning, input sequences need to be padded to the same length within a batch to enable parallel processing. Padding involves appending a special token (<|endoftext|>) or its corresponding token ID to the shorter sequences.

Custom Collate Function: Initial Implementation

A basic custom collate function pads sequences to the maximum length within a batch.

```
def custom_collate_fn(batch, pad_token_id=50256, device="cpu"):
    """
    Custom collate function for padding sequences in a batch.

    Args:
        batch (list): A list of tokenized sequences.
        pad_token_id (int): The token ID used for padding.
        device (str): The device to move tensors to (e.g., "cpu" or "cuda").

    Returns:
        torch.Tensor: Padded Input Tensors.
    """
```

```
    # Determine the maximum sequence length in the batch
    batch_max_length = max(len(item) + 1 for item in batch)
    inputs_lst = []

    for item in batch:
        # Copy the sequence and add a padding token
        new_item = item.copy() + [pad_token_id]
        padded = new_item + [pad_token_id] * (batch_max_length - len(new_item))
        inputs = torch.tensor(padded[:-1])  # Input IDs
        inputs_lst.append(inputs)

    # Stack the padded sequences into a tensor
    inputs_tensor = torch.stack(inputs_lst).to(device)
    return inputs_tensor
```

Testing the Function

```
# Sample inputs
inputs_1 = [0, 1, 2, 3, 4]
inputs_2 = [5, 6]
inputs_3 = [7, 8, 9]

# Batch of inputs
batch = [inputs_1, inputs_2, inputs_3]

# Apply the collate function
print(custom_collate_fn(batch))
```

Output:

```
tensor ([[    0,     1,     2,     3,     4],
         [    5,     6, 50256, 50256, 50256],
         [    7,     8,     9, 50256, 50256]])
```

Enhanced Collate Function: Adding Target Sequences

To compute the loss during training, we need to create target sequences where tokens are shifted one position to the right. Additionally, padding tokens should be excluded from loss calculation.

```
def custom_collate_fn_with_targets(
    batch, pad_token_id=50256, ignore_index=-100, device="cpu"
):
    """
    Custom collate function to create input and Target Tensors with padding.
    Args:
        batch (list): A list of tokenized sequences.
        pad_token_id (int): The token ID used for padding.


        ignore_index (int): Value used to ignore certain tokens during loss calculation.
        device (str): The device to move tensors to.

    Returns:
        tuple: A tuple containing input and Target Tensors.
    """
    batch_max_length = max(len(item) + 1 for item in batch)
    inputs_lst, targets_lst = [], []

    for item in batch:
        # Create input and target sequences
        new_item = item.copy() + [pad_token_id]
        padded = new_item + [pad_token_id] * (batch_max_length - len(new_item))
        inputs = torch.tensor(padded[:-1])  # Input IDs
        targets = torch.tensor(padded[1:])  # Target IDs
        # Mask padding tokens in the Target Tensor
        targets[targets == pad_token_id] = ignore_index
```

```
        inputs_lst.append(inputs)
        targets_lst.append(targets)

    # Stack inputs and targets into tensors
    inputs_tensor = torch.stack(inputs_lst).to(device)
    targets_tensor = torch.stack(targets_lst).to(device)
    return inputs_tensor, targets_tensor
```

Final Collate Function with Sequence Length Limiting

For larger datasets, it's essential to limit sequence lengths to fit within the model's context window.

```
def custom_collate_fn_with_limit(
        batch, pad_token_id=50256, ignore_index=-100, allowed_max_length=1024,
        device="cpu"
):
    """
    Collate function with sequence length limiting for large datasets.

    Args:
        allowed_max_length (int): Maximum allowed sequence length.
    """
    batch_max_length = min(max(len(item) + 1 for item in batch), allowed_max_length)
    inputs_lst, targets_lst = [], []

    for item in batch:
        new_item = item.copy() + [pad_token_id]
        padded = new_item + [pad_token_id] * (batch_max_length - len(new_item))
        inputs = torch.tensor(padded[:-1])
        targets = torch.tensor(padded[1:])
        targets[targets == pad_token_id] = ignore_index
        inputs_lst.append(inputs[:allowed_max_length])
```

```
        targets_lst.append(targets[:allowed_max_length])

    inputs_tensor = torch.stack(inputs_lst).to(device)
    targets_tensor = torch.stack(targets_lst).to(device)
    return inputs_tensor, targets_tensor
```

Some Best Practices during this process:

1. Dynamic Padding: Padding is applied only up to the length of the longest sequence in the batch, minimizing unnecessary computations.
2. Ignoring Padding Tokens: Padding tokens are excluded from the loss calculation using ignore_index=-100 to ensure meaningful tokens contribute to training.
3. Retaining Special Tokens: The <|endoftext|> token is preserved in the target sequence to help the model learn response completion.
4. Sequence Length Limitation: Restricting sequences to the model's context window (e.g., 1024 tokens for GPT-2) ensures compatibility with large datasets.
5. Focus on Response Generation: By optionally masking instruction tokens, models can focus on generating accurate responses, reducing overfitting.

7.4 Setting Up Data Loaders for Instruction-Based Datasets

After successfully implementing the Instruction Dataset class and the custom_collate_fn function, we are ready to integrate them into PyTorch data loaders. These data loaders will handle shuffling and batching of the dataset, streamlining the Fine-tuning process for a pretrained Large Language Model (LLM).

Setting the Device for Data Processing

To optimize performance, we need to specify the device where the data will be processed. Depending on the hardware, this can be a CPU, a GPU (using CUDA), or an Apple Silicon device (using MPS). Moving data to the appropriate device within the custom_collate_fn ensures that the data transfer happens in the background, minimizing overhead during training.

```
import torch
# Initialize the device based on hardware availability
device = torch.device("cuda" if torch.cuda.is_available() else "cpu")
# Uncomment the following lines for Apple Silicon (MPS) support if needed
```

```
# if torch.backends.mps.is_available():
#     device = torch.device("mps")
print("Device:", device)
```

Example Output:

```
Device: cuda
```

Creating a Partial Function for Collate Function Customization

Using Python's functools.partial, we prefill the device and allowed_max_length parameters in the custom_collate_fn. This simplifies the function's usage when passed to the DataLoader.

```
from functools import partial
# Customize the collate function with predefined parameters
customized_collate_fn = partial(
    custom_collate_fn,
    device=device,
    allowed_max_length=1024  # Set maximum sequence length
)
```

Setting Up Data Loaders

Using PyTorch's DataLoader, we create loaders for the training, validation, and test datasets. The InstructionDataset class handles tokenization, and the customized_collate_fn manages batching and padding.

```
from torch.utils.data import DataLoader
# Parameters for data loading
num_workers = 0  # Number of subprocesses for data loading
batch_size = 8   # Number of samples per batch
torch.manual_seed(123)  # Ensure reproducibility

# Training dataset and loader
train_dataset = InstructionDataset(train_data, tokenizer)
train_loader = DataLoader(
    train_dataset,
```

```
    batch_size=batch_size,
    collate_fn=customized_collate_fn,
    shuffle=True,      # Shuffle data for training
    drop_last=True,    # Drop the last incomplete batch
    num_workers=num_workers
)

# Validation dataset and loader
val_dataset = InstructionDataset(val_data, tokenizer)
val_loader = DataLoader(
    val_dataset,
    batch_size=batch_size,
    collate_fn=customized_collate_fn,
    shuffle=False,      # No shuffling for validation
    drop_last=False,    # Retain all batches
    num_workers=num_workers
)

# Test dataset and loader
test_dataset = InstructionDataset(test_data, tokenizer)
test_loader = DataLoader(
    test_dataset,
    batch_size=batch_size,
    collate_fn=customized_collate_fn,
    shuffle=False,      # No shuffling for testing
    drop_last=False,    # Retain all batches
    num_workers=num_workers
)
```

Inspecting the Data Loader Outputs

The following code snippet checks the dimensions of the input and target batches generated by the training loader. This ensures the batching process is functioning as expected.

```
print("Train loader:")
for inputs, targets in train_loader:
    print(f"Inputs shape: {inputs.shape}, Targets shape: {targets.shape}")
```

Example Output:

```
Train loader:
Inputs shape: torch.Size([8, 45]), Targets shape: torch.Size([8, 45])
Inputs shape: torch.Size([8, 52]), Targets shape: torch.Size([8, 52])
Inputs shape: torch.Size([8, 63]), Targets shape: torch.Size([8, 63])
```

...

1. **Batch Dimensions:**
   - o The first dimension corresponds to the batch size (e.g., 8).
   - o The second dimension is the number of tokens, which varies per batch.
2. **Dynamic Padding:**
   - o Thanks to the custom_collate_fn, each batch is padded to the length of its longest sequence. This minimizes padding and optimizes training efficiency.
3. **Device Compatibility:**
   - o The data tensors are automatically transferred to the specified device (cpu, cuda, or mps).

Benefits of Custom Data Loaders

- Dynamic Length Handling: Batches have varying sequence lengths, reducing memory waste and computational overhead.
- Device Transfer Optimization: Data transfer occurs in the background, keeping the GPU available for model training.
- Scalability: The data loaders are ready to handle large datasets and integrate seamlessly with the LLM Fine-tuning workflow.

This setup prepares the data pipeline for training the LLM, ensuring that batches are efficiently created, padded, and transferred to the appropriate device. The next step involves loading the pretrained LLM and initiating the Fine-tuning process.

7.5 Loading a Pretrained Language Model

Instruction Fine-Tuning is a critical process that equips a pretrained GPT model with the ability to accurately interpret and respond to task-specific instructions. This guide elaborates on the steps involved in loading a pretrained model, assessing its baseline performance, and preparing it for Fine-tuning.

Why Use a Larger Model?

Smaller models like GPT-2 Small (124M parameters) often lack the capacity to handle nuanced and intricate instruction-following tasks. A medium-sized model with 355 million parameters (GPT-2 Medium) offers a better trade-off between computational feasibility and capability, making it more suitable for tasks requiring complex reasoning and generation.

The following code demonstrates how to load the pretrained GPT-2 Medium model:

```
from gpt_download import download_and_load_gpt2
from chapter04 import GPTModel
from chapter05 import load_weights_into_gpt

# Define the base configuration for the GPT model
BASE_CONFIG = {
    "vocab_size": 50257,        # Size of the vocabulary
    "context_length": 1024,     # Maximum number of tokens in input
    "drop_rate": 0.0,           # Dropout rate for regularization
    "qkv_bias": True            # Enable bias in attention mechanisms
}
# Configuration settings for various GPT-2 model sizes
model_configs = {
    "gpt2-small (124M)": {"emb_dim": 768, "n_layers": 12, "n_heads": 12},
    "gpt2-medium (355M)": {"emb_dim": 1024, "n_layers": 24, "n_heads": 16},
    "gpt2-large (774M)": {"emb_dim": 1280, "n_layers": 36, "n_heads": 20},
    "gpt2-xl (1558M)": {"emb_dim": 1600, "n_layers": 48, "n_heads": 25},
```

```
}
# Choose the GPT-2 model for Fine-tuning
CHOOSE_MODEL = "gpt2-medium (355M)"
BASE_CONFIG.update(model_configs[CHOOSE_MODEL])
# Extract the model size (e.g., "355M") from the selection
model_size = CHOOSE_MODEL.split(" ")[-1].strip("()")
# Download the pretrained GPT-2 weights and configurations
settings, params = download_and_load_gpt2(
    model_size=model_size,
    models_dir="gpt2"  # Directory to save the model files
)

# Initialize the GPT model using the configuration
model = GPTModel(BASE_CONFIG)

# Load the pretrained weights into the initialized model
load_weights_into_gpt(model, params)

# Set the model to evaluation mode
model.eval()

print("GPT-2 Medium model loaded successfully.")
```

Files Downloaded During Model Setup

The following files are downloaded:

- Model Checkpoints: Contain the pretrained weights.
- Vocabulary Files: Enable tokenization and detokenization.
- Configuration Files: Provide model specifications like layer count and embedding size.

Importance of Baseline Evaluation

Before Fine-tuning, it is crucial to assess the pretrained model's performance on a validation task. This establishes a reference point, helping us quantify improvements after Fine-tuning.

Validation Task Example

Consider a task requiring the conversion of an active voice sentence into passive voice.

Validation Input:

Below is an instruction that describes a task. Write a response that appropriately completes the request.

```
### Instruction:Convert the active sentence to passive: 'The chef cooks the meal every
    day.'

torch.manual_seed(123)  # Set a random seed for reproducibility

# Format the first validation example into the input format
input_text = format_input(val_data[0])
print("Input Text:\n", input_text)

# Generate a response using the pretrained model
from chapter05 import generate, text_to_token_ids, token_ids_to_text

# Tokenize the input and generate predictions
token_ids = generate(
    model=model,
    idx=text_to_token_ids(input_text, tokenizer),  # Convert input text to token IDs
    max_new_tokens=35,                        # Limit the response length
    context_size=BASE_CONFIG["context_length"],  # Use model's context length
    eos_id=50256                          # End-of-sequence token ID
)
```

```
# Convert the generated tokens back into human-readable text
generated_text = token_ids_to_text(token_ids, tokenizer)
```

Extracting the Model's Response

Since the generate function returns both the input and the generated output concatenated, we isolate the model's response by subtracting the length of the input text:

```
# Extract the generated response from the full text
response_text = generated_text[len(input_text):].strip()
print("Generated Response:\n", response_text)
```

Example Output:

```
### Response:
The chef cooks the meal every day.
### Instruction:
Convert the active sentence to passive: 'The chef cooks the
```

Observations from Baseline Evaluation

1. **Model's Behavior:** The model repeats the input text and part of the instruction, but fails to perform the task (i.e., converting active to passive voice).
2. **Limitation of Pretraining:** Pretrained models are designed for generic text generation and lack task-specific capabilities.
3. **Need for Fine-tuning:** Fine-tuning aligns the model with specific objectives, such as instruction comprehension and accurate response generation.

Goals of Fine-tuning

- Task-Specific Training: Teach the model to follow diverse instructions effectively.
- Performance Enhancement: Improve the quality and relevance of generated responses.
- Generalization: Ensure the model adapts to varied instruction formats and tasks.

In the next steps, we proceed with Fine-tuning the model to address its limitations, focusing on transforming its capabilities for targeted instruction-following tasks. Fine-tuning will involve leveraging our prepared dataset, custom collates functions, and optimised training strategies to achieve this goal.

7.6 Training the LLM on Instructional Data

The Fine-tuning process further trains a pretrained GPT model using an instruction dataset to improve its ability to understand and respond to specific instructions. This section outlines the steps involved, including initializing the Fine-tuning process, tracking loss metrics, and generating example responses to evaluate the model's progress.

Step 1: Initializing the Fine-tuning Process

We begin by loading the pretrained model onto the appropriate device and calculating the initial training and validation losses. This provides a baseline to assess the impact of Fine-tuning.

Code to Calculate Initial Loss

```
import calc_loss_loader


# Move the model to the selected device (CPU or GPU)
model.to(device)


# Set a random seed for reproducibility
torch.manual_seed(123)


# Calculate initial training and validation losses
with torch.no_grad():
    train_loss = calc_loss_loader(
        train_loader, model, device, num_batches=5  # Evaluate on 5 training batches
    )
    val_loss = calc_loss_loader(
        val_loader, model, device, num_batches=5  # Evaluate on 5 validation batches
    )
print("Initial Training Loss:", train_loss)
print("Initial Validation Loss:", val_loss)
```

Output:

Initial Training Loss: 3.825908660888672

Initial Validation Loss: 3.7619335651397705

Step 2: Training the Model

Optimizer Initialization

We use the AdamW optimizer, which is well-suited for transformer-based models, with a small learning rate and weight decay for regularization.

```
import torch.optim


# Initialize the optimizer
optimizer = torch.optim.AdamW(
    model.parameters(), lr=0.00005, weight_decay=0.1
)
```

Training Configuration

The train_model_simple function handles the training loop, validation, and evaluation. This function tracks training and validation losses at regular intervals and generates example responses based on validation data.

```
import train_model_simple
import time
# Start timing the training process
start_time = time.time()


# Set training parameters
num_epochs = 2  # Number of epochs for training
eval_freq = 5   # Evaluate every 5 batches
eval_iter = 5   # Number of iterations for evaluation


# Train the model and capture training progress
train_losses, val_losses, tokens_seen = train_model_simple(
```

```
    model, train_loader, val_loader, optimizer, device,
    num_epochs=num_epochs, eval_freq=eval_freq, eval_iter=eval_iter,
    start_context=format_input(val_data[0]), tokenizer=tokenizer
)

# Calculate and display total execution time
end_time = time.time()
execution_time_minutes = (end_time - start_time) / 60
print(f"Training completed in {execution_time_minutes:.2f} minutes.")
```

Example Training Output

The training progress is displayed at regular intervals, showing the training and validation loss values, along with generated example responses.

Output:

```
Epoch 1 (Step 000005): Train Loss 1.174, Val Loss 1.103
Epoch 1 (Step 000010): Train Loss 0.872, Val Loss 0.944
Epoch 1 (Step 000115): Train Loss 0.520, Val Loss 0.665
Example Response:
Instruction: Convert the active sentence to passive: 'The chef cooks the meal every day.'
Response: The meal is cooked every day by the chef.<|endoftext|>
...
Epoch 2 (Step 000230): Train Loss 0.300, Val Loss 0.657
Training completed in 0.87 minutes.
```

Step 3: Evaluating Training Progress

Observing Loss Trends

The loss values consistently decrease over epochs, indicating that the model is learning effectively. The rapid decrease in early epochs suggests the model is quickly grasping meaningful patterns, while slower reductions later suggest convergence.

Step 4: Visualizing Loss Metrics

To gain deeper insights into the training process, we plot the training and validation losses over time.

```
import plot_losses

# Create a tensor for epoch values
epochs_tensor = torch.linspace(0, num_epochs, len(train_losses))

# Plot the loss curves
plot_losses(epochs_tensor, tokens_seen, train_losses, val_losses)
```

Step 5: Assessing Response Quality

While loss metrics are valuable, the most important aspect is the quality of the generated responses. Fine-tuning improves the model's ability to generate accurate, contextually relevant outputs. For example:

Pre-Fine-tuning Response:

Instruction:

Convert the active sentence to passive: 'The chef cooks the meal every day.'

Response:

The chef cooks the meal every day.

The model fails to perform the task and merely repeats part of the input.

Post-Fine-tuning Response:

Instruction:

Convert the active sentence to passive: 'The chef cooks the meal every day.'

Response:

The meal is cooked every day by the chef.

The fine-tuned model correctly converts the sentence into passive voice, showcasing improved instruction-following capability.

Improvements in Fine-tuning

1. **Efficient Training Process:** The train_model_simple function simplifies tracking progress and evaluating the model.
2. **Dynamic Evaluation:** Frequent loss calculations and response generation during training ensure real-time assessment of improvements.
3. **Optimized Parameters:** Using a small learning rate and weight decay prevents overfitting while ensuring stable convergence.
4. **Hardware Considerations:** For faster training, using GPUs (like NVIDIA A100) significantly reduces training time. Cloud-based GPUs are viable alternatives for resource-constrained environments.
5. **Balanced Training:** Two epochs are sufficient to achieve strong results, preventing overfitting while maximising model performance.

Fine-tuning transforms a generic pretrained GPT model into a task-specific tool capable of understanding and following complex instructions with high accuracy.

7.7 Extracting and Saving Output Responses

After Fine-tuning the model on the training set, the next step is to evaluate its performance using the held-out test set. This involves generating responses for test set inputs, comparing them with expected outputs, and quantitatively assessing the model's ability to follow instructions. To efficiently assess performance, we use automated conversational evaluation inspired by benchmarks like AlpacaEval, enabling scalable and targeted analysis.

Step 1: Generating Responses for the Test Set

The goal is to generate responses for each input in the test dataset and compare them with the expected answers. This step provides insights into the model's ability to handle instructions and generate accurate outputs.

```
import torch
from tqdm import tqdm  # For progress visualization


# Generate responses for all entries in the test set
torch.manual_seed(123)  # Ensure reproducibility


for i, entry in tqdm(enumerate(test_data), total=len(test_data)):
```

```
    # Format the input text for the model
    input_text = format_input(entry)

    # Generate response using the fine-tuned model
    token_ids = generate(
        model=model,
        idx=text_to_token_ids(input_text, tokenizer).to(device),  # Tokenize input
        max_new_tokens=256,                          # Limit response length
      context_size=BASE_CONFIG["context_length"],         # Context length of the model
        eos_id=50256                               # End-of-sequence token ID
    )

    # Decode generated tokens into text
    generated_text = token_ids_to_text(token_ids, tokenizer)

    # Extract the response portion from the generated text
    response_text = (
        generated_text[len(input_text):] # Remove input portion
        .replace("### Response:", "")      # Remove response prefix
        .strip()                    # Clean up whitespace
    )

    # Add the generated response to the test data
    test_data[i]["model_response"] = response_text
```

Step 2: Saving and Verifying Responses

After generating responses for all test entries, save the updated dataset to a JSON file for record-keeping and later analysis.

```
import json

# Save the updated test set with model responses
with open("instruction-data-with-response.json", "w") as file:
```

```
    json.dump(test_data, file, indent=4)  # Save with indentation for readability
print("Responses saved to 'instruction-data-with-response.json'.")
```

Check the structure of the updated test data to ensure the responses were correctly appended.

```
# Display an example entry from the updated test set
print(test_data[0])
```

Example Output:

```
{
    "instruction": "Rewrite the sentence using a simile.",
    "input": "The car is very fast.",
    "output": "The car is as fast as lightning.",
    "model_response": "The car is as fast as a bullet."
}
```

Step 3: Comparing Responses for Manual Analysis

Manually compare the first few model responses with the expected outputs for a qualitative assessment.

```
# Compare model responses with expected outputs for sample entries
for entry in test_data[:3]:
    input_text = format_input(entry)
    print(input_text)
    print(f"\nExpected Response:\n>> {entry['output']}")
    print(f"\nModel Response:\n>> {entry['model_response']}")
    print("-------------------------------------")
```

Example Output:

Instruction: Rewrite the sentence using a simile.

Input: The car is very fast.

Expected Response: The car is as fast as lightning.

Model Response: The car is as fast as a bullet.

Instruction: What type of cloud is typically associated with thunderstorms?

Input:

Expected Response:The type of cloud typically associated with thunderstorms is cumulonimbus.

Model Response: The type of cloud associated with thunderstorms is a cumulus cloud.

Instruction: Name the author of 'Pride and Prejudice.'

Input:

Expected Response: Jane Austen.

Model Response: The author of 'Pride and Prejudice' is Jane Austen.

Step 4: Automated Evaluation Using Another LLM

Manual evaluation is insightful but time-intensive, especially for large datasets. Using another LLM to evaluate responses automates the process, saving resources while maintaining objectivity. Append the responses to the dataset to prepare them for automated evaluation. A more advanced setup would involve scoring responses based on their alignment with expected answers.

Step 5: Saving the Fine-Tuned Model

Save the fine-tuned model for future use to avoid re-training and to enable testing on new datasets.

```
import re
# Generate a filename for the fine-tuned model
file_name = f"{re.sub(r'[ ()]', '', CHOOSE_MODEL)}-sft.pth"

# Save the model's state dictionary
torch.save(model.state_dict(), file_name)

print(f"Model saved as {file_name}")
```

Example Output:

Model saved as gpt2-medium355M-sft.pth

1. **Response Quality:** The model performs well for many tasks but occasionally generates responses that are close but not entirely correct.

   Example: Misidentifying "cumulus clouds" as the type associated with thunderstorms instead of "cumulonimbus clouds."

2. **Strengths:** The model handles tasks with well-defined patterns (e.g., passive-to-active conversion, author identification).

3. **Challenges:** Tasks requiring nuanced understanding or specific knowledge may need additional Fine-tuning or more diverse datasets.

4. **Automated Evaluation Benefits:** Streamlines large-scale evaluation. Reduces dependency on human reviewers.

Future Directions

1. **Advanced Evaluation Metrics:** Use BLEU, ROUGE, or METEOR to score generated responses. Employ human preference scores for qualitative insights.

2. **Further Fine-tuning:** Include domain-specific datasets for better generalization in specialized tasks.

3. **Real-World Testing:** Test the model on live user interactions to gauge practical utility.

This approach ensures the fine-tuned LLM is thoroughly evaluated and ready for deployment in instruction-following tasks.

7.8 Evaluating the Performance of the Fine-Tuned Model

Evaluating the performance of a fine-tuned LLM on a test set manually is labor-intensive and does not scale well for large datasets. Automating this process using a larger and more advanced LLM provides a scalable, consistent, and detailed evaluation of the generated responses. In this example, we use an 8-billion-parameter Llama 3 model, deployed via the open-source Ollama application, to assess the responses generated by the fine-tuned LLM.

Step 1: Setting Up the Llama 3 Model with Ollama

Installing and Running Ollama

1. **Installation:**
   - Visit Ollama's official website and follow the installation instructions for your operating system.
   - For macOS and Windows, open the Ollama application and enable command-line access if prompted.
   - For Linux, use the installation command provided on the Ollama website.
2. **Running the Llama 3 Model Locally:**
   - Start the Ollama service by running ollama serve in a terminal or through the Ollama application.
   - Use the command ollama run llama3 to interact with the model. The model will be downloaded the first time you execute this command (approximately 4.7 GB).
3. **Example Interaction with Llama 3:**
   - After starting the service, try asking the model a question:

     >>> What do llamas eat?

     Llamas are ruminant animals... (response varies)
   - End the session by typing /bye.

Step 2: Verifying Ollama's Availability in Python

Before evaluating the test set responses, ensure the Ollama service is running.

Code to Check Ollama's Status

```
import psutil

def check_if_running(process_name):
    """Check if a specific process is running on the system."""
    running = False
    for proc in psutil.process_iter(["name"]):
        if process_name in proc.info["name"]:
```

```
            running = True
            break
    return running

# Verify if Ollama is running
ollama_running = check_if_running("ollama")
if not ollama_running:
    raise RuntimeError("Ollama not running. Launch Ollama before proceeding.")

print("Ollama running:", ollama_running
)
```

Example Output:

```
Ollama running: True
```

Step 3: Interfacing with Llama 3 Using a REST API

The Ollama service provides a REST API for querying the Llama 3 model programmatically.

API Query Function

```
import json
import urllib.request

def query_model(prompt, model="llama3", url="http://localhost:11434/api/chat"):
    """Query the Llama 3 model via Ollama's REST API."""
    data = {
        "model": model,
        "messages": [{"role": "user", "content": prompt}],
        "options": {
            "seed": 123,          # Set a fixed seed for reproducibility
            "temperature": 0,     # Deterministic response
            "num_ctx": 2048       # Context length
        }
```

```
    }
    payload = json.dumps(data).encode("utf-8")
    request = urllib.request.Request(url, data=payload, method="POST")
    request.add_header("Content-Type", "application/json")

    response_data = ""
    with urllib.request.urlopen(request) as response:
        while True:
            line = response.readline().decode("utf-8")
            if not line:
                break
            response_json = json.loads(line)
            response_data += response_json["message"]["content"]
    return response_data
```

Example Query to Llama 3

```
model = "llama3"
result = query_model("What do llamas eat?", model)
print(result)
```

Output:

Llamas are ruminant animals, which means they have a four-chambered stomach...

Step 4: Scoring the Test Set Responses

The larger LLM evaluates responses generated by the fine-tuned model on a scale from 0 to 100, comparing them with the expected outputs.

Evaluate Sample Test Set Responses

```
for entry in test_data[:3]:
    # Create a detailed evaluation prompt
    prompt = (
        f"Given the input `{format_input(entry)}` "
        f"and correct output `{entry['output']}`, "
```

```
        f"score the model response `{entry['model_response']}` "
        f"on a scale from 0 to 100, where 100 is the best score."
    )
    print("\nDataset Response:")
    print(">>", entry['output'])
    print("\nModel Response:")
    print(">>", entry["model_response"])
    print("\nScore:")
    print(">>", query_model(prompt))
    print("\n-------------------------")
```

Example Output:

```
Dataset Response:
>> The car is as fast as lightning.

Model Response:
>> The car is as fast as a bullet.

Score:
>> 85
-------------------------
```

Step 5: Automating the Scoring Process

To automate the scoring for the entire test dataset, use the following function:

```
from tqdm import tqdm
def generate_model_scores(json_data, json_key, model="llama3"):
    """Generate scores for model responses using Llama 3."""
    scores = []
    for entry in tqdm(json_data, desc="Scoring entries"):
        prompt = (
            f"Given the input `{format_input(entry)}` "
```

```
        f"and correct output `{entry['output']}`, "
        f"score the model response `{entry[json_key]}` "
        f"on a scale from 0 to 100. Respond with the integer number only."
    )
    score = query_model(prompt, model)
    try:
        scores.append(int(score))
    except ValueError:
        print(f"Could not convert score: {score}")
        continue
  return scores
```

Apply the Scoring Function

```
scores = generate_model_scores(test_data, "model_response")
print(f"Number of scores: {len(scores)} of {len(test_data)}")
print(f"Average score: {sum(scores)/len(scores):.2f}")
```

Output:

```
Number of scores: 110 of 110
Average score: 75.12
```

Step 6: Saving the Evaluated Model

Finally, save the fine-tuned model for future use.

```
import re
# Generate a filename for the saved model
file_name = f"{re.sub(r'[ ()]', '', CHOOSE_MODEL)}-sft.pth"
# Save the model's state dictionary
torch.save(model.state_dict(), file_name)
print(f"Model saved as {file_name}")
```

Output:

```
Model saved as gpt2-medium355M-sft.pth
```

Key Takeaways and Future Directions

1. Evaluation Insights:
   - o Automated scoring reveals strengths and weaknesses in the fine-tuned model's ability to follow instructions.
   - o Example scores range from high for accurate responses to low for incorrect answers.
2. Scalability:
   - o Using Llama 3 for evaluation enables large-scale assessment without manual effort.
3. Improvement Strategies:
   - o Experiment with hyperparameters, dataset size, and instruction diversity.
   - o Consider using a larger pretrained model for enhanced capacity.

This approach ensures the fine-tuned model is rigorously evaluated and ready for practical applications in instruction-following tasks.

In this chapter, we delved into the Fine-tuning process for Large Language Models (LLMs) to enhance their ability to follow instructions effectively. Beginning with data preparation, we designed an instruction dataset with examples containing input-output pairs. The dataset was formatted into a prompt-response structure tailored to guide the model during training. Leveraging pre-existing functionalities for loss calculation and training, we fine-tuned a pretrained GPT-2 Medium model on this dataset, significantly improving its performance on instruction-following tasks.

We evaluated the fine-tuned model's outputs against a held-out test set to assess its learning. While manual evaluation provided insights into specific cases, it was insufficient for large datasets. To scale the evaluation, we used an automated scoring approach with a larger, instruction-fine-tuned Llama 3 model via the Ollama application. This enabled consistent, quantitative assessment, assigning scores to model-generated responses based on their alignment with reference outputs. The average test set score provided a benchmark for performance, guiding future improvements.

The chapter highlighted the challenges and nuances of Instruction Fine-Tuning, including dataset design, hyperparameter tuning, and evaluation scalability. It also demonstrated how automated tools can streamline assessment. With these methodologies, LLMs can be further refined for specific use cases, ensuring adaptability and accuracy in real-world applications.

SUMMARY

✓ This chapter focused on enhancing Large Language Models (LLMs) through Instruction Fine-Tuning, building on foundational Pretraining and classification tasks to enable better understanding and execution of specific human instructions.

✓ The process began with preparing high-quality instruction-response datasets, formatted into prompt-response structures to train the model on tasks like grammar correction, style transformation, summarization, and question answering.

✓ Custom batching strategies, including dynamic padding, token masking, and sequence length limiting, were implemented to optimize data handling during Fine-tuning, ensuring efficient training and scalability for large datasets.

✓ A pretrained GPT-2 Medium model with 355 million parameters was loaded, evaluated on baseline tasks, and fine-tuned using supervised methods to minimize the discrepancy between generated outputs and expected responses.

✓ Training progress was monitored using metrics like training and validation losses, dynamic evaluation on validation examples, and visualizing loss trends to ensure stable convergence and improved performance.

✓ To evaluate the fine-tuned model's performance at scale, automated assessment was conducted using a larger LLM (Llama 3), which scored model responses based on alignment with expected outputs, streamlining the evaluation process.

✓ The chapter emphasized strategies for improving instruction-following capabilities, such as dataset diversification, parameter optimization, and leveraging automated evaluation tools, enabling LLMs to perform effectively in diverse real-world applications.

Exercises

Exercise 1 – Multiple Choice Questions

1. What is the primary purpose of Instruction Fine-Tuning in LLMs?
   a) Improve grammar accuracy
   b) Enhance the ability to follow and execute specific instructions
   c) Increase the vocabulary size of the model
   d) Enable the model to generate poetry
2. During Instruction Fine-Tuning, padding tokens are excluded from the loss calculation. What parameter is typically used to ignore padding tokens?
   a) pad_token_id=50256 b) context_size=1024
   c) ignore_index=-100 d) eos_id=50256

Exercise 2 – One Word Answers

1. What technique is commonly used during Fine-tuning to minimize discrepancies between generated outputs and expected responses?
2. Which evaluation metric assigns scores to generated responses based on alignment with reference outputs?

Exercise 3 – Short Answers

1. Why is it essential to limit the sequence length during Instruction Fine-Tuning?
2. How does automated evaluation using larger models like Llama 3 improve scalability?

Exercise 4 – Long Answers

1. Explain the process of instruction Fine-tuning and its significance in improving LLMs.
2. Discuss the role of evaluation during instruction Fine-tuning and how automated tools are leveraged for large datasets.

Answers

Exercise 1- 1) b, 2) c

Exercise 2- 1) Supervised, 2) Automated

Online Resources

	Practice Paper	YouTube Video Playlist Link
Link	https://forms.gle/stPFe8JGzgePo5hj6	https://www.youtube.com/ playlist?list=PLzlh_31VWEFrErzm 4fzFcG6sk5USbVF-I
QR Code		

Chapter 8

INTRODUCTION TO PYTORCH

In this chapter you will learn about:

- ☐ What is PyTorch?
- ☐ Why Choose PyTorch for Deep Learning?
- ☐ Key Features of PyTorch
- ☐ PyTorch in Action: A Simple Deep Learning Workflow

Deep Learning, a subcategory of Machine Learning, focuses on developing and utilising deep neural networks to solve complex tasks such as Image Recognition, Natural Language Processing, and Autonomous Systems. PyTorch, developed by Facebook's AI Research (FAIR) lab, has become one of the leading frameworks for implementing deep learning models. Its flexibility, dynamic computation graph, and ease of use have made it a favourite among researchers and practitioners alike. This article introduces PyTorch, its key features, and why it is ideal for deep learning applications.

8.1 What is PyTorch?

PyTorch is an open-source deep learning framework primarily used for building and training neural networks. Released in 2016, PyTorch provides a Pythonic interface, making it intuitive for Python developers. Its dynamic computation graph allows for real-time debugging and flexibility in model building, distinguishing it from its predecessor frameworks like TensorFlow (which originally relied on static graphs).

PyTorch supports multiple Machine Learning workflows, including supervised, unsupervised, and reinforcement learning, making it versatile for a variety of deep learning applications.

8.2 Key Features of PyTorch

8.2.1. Dynamic Computation Graphs

PyTorch's dynamic computation graph is one of its standout features. Unlike static graphs, which require the entire computation graph to be defined before execution, dynamic graphs are created on the fly. This means that you can modify the graph during runtime, which is particularly useful for models that involve variable-length inputs or complex architectures such as recursive neural networks.

8.2.2. Autograd: Automatic Differentiation

PyTorch includes a module called Autograd, which provides automatic differentiation for all operations on tensors. It records the operations performed on tensors to create a computation graph dynamically. During backpropagation, Autograd computes gradients automatically, simplifying the process of optimizing neural networks.

Example:

```
import torch
# Create tensors
x = torch.tensor(2.0, requires_grad=True)
y = x**2 + 3*x + 1

# Compute gradients
y.backward()
print(x.grad)  # Output: 7.0
```

8.2.3. Tensor Computation

At its core, PyTorch is built around tensors, which are multi-dimensional arrays similar to NumPy arrays. Tensors are the building blocks of neural networks and support GPU acceleration, making PyTorch ideal for computationally intensive deep learning tasks.

Example:

```
# Tensor creation
tensor = torch.tensor([[1, 2], [3, 4]], dtype=torch.float32)
print(tensor)

# Tensor operations
tensor_sum = tensor.sum()
print(tensor_sum)
```

8.2.4. Seamless GPU Acceleration

PyTorch provides native support for GPU computation. Tensors and models can be easily transferred between CPUs and GPUs with minimal code changes.

Example:

```
device = torch.device("cuda" if torch.cuda.is_available() else "cpu")
tensor = torch.tensor([1.0, 2.0, 3.0], device=device)
print(tensor)
```

8.2.5. Torch.nn for Neural Networks

The torch.nn module in PyTorch simplifies defining, training, and evaluating neural networks. It provides pre-built layers, such as fully connected, convolutional, and recurrent layers, which can be easily combined to create complex architectures.

Example of a simple Feed-Forward Neural Network:

```
import torch.nn as nn
class SimpleNN(nn.Module):
    def __init__(self):
        super(SimpleNN, self).__init__()
        self.fc1 = nn.Linear(10, 5)
```

```
    self.fc2 = nn.Linear(5, 1)
  def forward(self, x):
    x = torch.relu(self.fc1(x))
    x = torch.sigmoid(self.fc2(x))
    return x
```

8.3 Why Choose PyTorch for Deep Learning?

8.3.1. Ease of Use

PyTorch's intuitive API allows developers to prototype models quickly. Its Pythonic design makes it accessible for both beginners and experienced programmers.

8.3.2. Flexibility

Dynamic graphs make PyTorch highly flexible for research and experimentation. Developers can modify models dynamically without needing to rebuild or retrain the entire graph.

8.3.3. Community and Ecosystem

PyTorch has a large and active community, ensuring a wealth of resources, tutorials, and libraries for developers. Libraries like TorchVision (for image processing), TorchText (for NLP), and TorchAudio (for audio processing) extend PyTorch's functionality for specific domains.

8.3.4. Interoperability with Python Libraries

PyTorch integrates seamlessly with Python libraries like NumPy, SciPy, and scikit-learn, enabling developers to leverage existing tools and workflows.

8.3.5. Production-Ready

With the release of TorchScript, PyTorch has bridged the gap between research and production. TorchScript allows PyTorch models to be exported and deployed in production environments efficiently.

8.4 PyTorch in Action: A Simple Deep Learning Workflow

1. Dataset Preparation

PyTorch provides utilities in the torch.utils.data module for loading and preprocessing datasets.

Example:

```
from torch.utils.data import DataLoader, Dataset

# Custom dataset
class CustomDataset(Dataset):
    def __init__(self):
        self.data = torch.randn(100, 10)
        self.labels = torch.randint(0, 2, (100,))

    def __len__(self):
        return len(self.data)

    def __getitem__(self, idx):
        return self.data[idx], self.labels[idx]

dataset = CustomDataset()
dataloader = DataLoader(dataset, batch_size=16, shuffle=True)
```

2. Model Building

Using the torch.nn module, you can define your deep learning model.

3. Training the Model

PyTorch provides tools for loss computation and optimization.

Example:

```
import torch.optim as optim
model = SimpleNN()
criterion = nn.BCELoss()  # Binary Cross-Entropy Loss
optimizer = optim.SGD(model.parameters(), lr=0.01)

for epoch in range(10):
    for data, labels in dataloader:
```

```
optimizer.zero_grad()  # Clear previous gradients
outputs = model(data)
loss = criterion(outputs.squeeze(), labels.float())
loss.backward()  # Backpropagation
optimizer.step()  # Update weights
```

8.5 Real-World Applications of PyTorch

8.5.1 Computer Vision

Computer vision is one of the most significant areas where PyTorch has made a considerable impact. It is used to solve complex visual recognition tasks such as object detection, image segmentation, and classification. PyTorch provides a seamless workflow for implementing computer vision models due to its flexibility and the support of TorchVision, a specialized library designed for image processing tasks.

- Object Detection: PyTorch simplifies object detection by enabling the use of pre-trained models such as Faster R-CNN and YOLO (You Only Look Once). These models can identify objects within an image and provide bounding boxes around them, making them essential for applications like autonomous driving and security systems.
- Image Segmentation: For tasks requiring pixel-level predictions, such as semantic segmentation (assigning a class label to each pixel in an image), PyTorch provides state-of-the-art architectures like Mask R-CNN and U-Net. These are widely used in medical imaging, where precise segmentation of tumors or organs is critical.
- Image Classification: With models like ResNet (Residual Networks) and DenseNet, PyTorch facilitates efficient image classification. These models classify entire images into predefined categories, a fundamental task in applications like facial recognition and visual search.
- Data Augmentation: The TorchVision library also includes tools for data preprocessing and augmentation, such as resizing, cropping, flipping, and rotating images, which help improve model robustness.

PyTorch's GPU support accelerates these computations, enabling researchers to handle large-scale datasets and train sophisticated models efficiently.

8.5.2 Natural Language Processing

Natural Language Processing (NLP) focuses on enabling machines to understand, interpret, and generate human language. PyTorch has become a key player in the

NLP domain due to its flexibility and compatibility with libraries like Hugging Face Transformers, which provide pre-trained models for advanced NLP tasks.

- Transformers: PyTorch is instrumental in implementing transformer-based architectures like BERT (Bidirectional Encoder Representations from Transformers), GPT (Generative Pre-trained Transformer), and T5 (Text-to-Text Transfer Transformer). These models excel in tasks such as text classification, sentiment analysis, machine translation, and summarisation.
- Sequence Modeling: PyTorch's native support for Recurrent Neural Networks (RNNs), Long Short-Term Memory Networks (LSTMs), and gated recurrent units (GRUs) allows it to process sequential data effectively. These architectures are particularly useful for tasks like speech recognition and language modelling.
- Custom Tokenization: The torchtext library provides tokenization utilities and datasets for NLP tasks, enabling researchers to preprocess text efficiently before feeding it into models.
- Speech-to-Text and Text-to-Speech: PyTorch, combined with libraries like Torchaudio, facilitates the development of speech recognition systems and text-to-speech conversion.

Fine-tuning and Transfer Learning: Hugging Face Transformers allow developers to fine-tune pre-trained models on specific datasets, significantly reducing the time and computational resources required for building NLP systems.

These capabilities make PyTorch a versatile framework for handling the complexities of human language understanding and generation.

8.5.3 Reinforcement Learning

Reinforcement Learning (RL) is a type of Machine Learning where agents learn to make decisions by interacting with an environment and receiving feedback in the form of rewards or penalties. PyTorch has emerged as a preferred choice for implementing RL algorithms due to its dynamic computation graph and support for gradient-based optimization.

- Frameworks for RL: PyTorch is integrated into popular RL frameworks like Stable-Baselines and RLlib, which provide a suite of pre-built algorithms such as Deep Q-Networks (DQN), Proximal Policy Optimization (PPO), and A3C (Asynchronous Advantage Actor-Critic).
- Simulation Environments: PyTorch models can be trained in simulation environments like OpenAI Gym or Unity ML-Agents, where agents interact with virtual worlds to learn optimal strategies.

- Policy-Based Learning: PyTorch supports policy gradient methods, where agents directly learn policies that map states to actions, making it suitable for continuous action spaces, such as robotics and autonomous navigation.
- Actor-Critic Models: Actor-Critic algorithms, which combine value-based and policy-based methods, are implemented seamlessly using PyTorch, enabling efficient learning of both state value functions and optimal policies.
- Applications of RL: PyTorch-powered RL has been applied in various domains, including gaming (e.g., training agents to play complex games like Go or StarCraft), robotics (e.g., teaching robots to navigate or manipulate objects), and financial modeling (e.g., optimizing trading strategies).

PyTorch's flexibility and GPU acceleration allow researchers to iterate quickly and efficiently train RL models in complex environments.

8.5.4 Generative Models

Generative models are a class of Machine Learning models designed to generate new data samples similar to a given dataset. PyTorch is widely used to implement and train generative models because it supports dynamic graphs and seamless gradient computation. The framework is particularly suited for developing Generative Adversarial Networks (GANs) and Variational AutoEncoders (VAEs), two of the most popular generative techniques.

- Generative Adversarial Networks (GANs): GANs consist of two neural networks—a generator and a discriminator—trained in a competitive manner. The generator learns to create realistic data samples, while the discriminator tries to differentiate between real and generated samples. PyTorch simplifies the process of implementing and training GANs, which are widely used in applications like:

  Image Generation: Generating high-quality images, such as realistic portraits, landscapes, and artwork.

  Style Transfer: Creating artistic images by transferring the style of one image onto another.

  Data Augmentation: Synthesizing new data samples to augment training datasets.

- Variational AutoEncoders (VAEs): VAEs are generative models that encode data into a latent space and decode it back to generate new samples. PyTorch makes it easy to define custom Encoder-Decoder architectures and optimize the associated loss functions. VAEs are used for:

  Anomaly Detection: Identifying unusual patterns in data, such as fraud detection or medical anomalies.

Image Synthesis: Generating diverse samples from a latent space for creative applications.

- Neural Style Transfer: PyTorch enables easy implementation of neural style transfer, which involves applying the style of one image to the content of another, resulting in unique artistic renditions.
- Audio and Video Generation: Beyond images, PyTorch is also used in generating realistic audio (e.g., speech synthesis) and video (e.g., creating deepfakes).

PyTorch's flexibility allows developers to experiment with novel generative architectures and train them efficiently, pushing the boundaries of what machines can create.

8.6 Limitations of PyTorch

While PyTorch has numerous strengths, it is not without limitations:

- Steeper Learning Curve: Beginners may initially find some advanced features challenging to grasp.
- Smaller Ecosystem for Mobile: TensorFlow currently supports mobile and embedded systems better.

PyTorch is a powerful and versatile framework for implementing deep learning models. Its dynamic computation graph, ease of use, and extensive community support make it a go-to choice for researchers and developers alike. Whether you're building state-of-the-art neural networks or experimenting with novel architectures, PyTorch provides the tools you need to succeed in deep learning.

SUMMARY

✓ PyTorch is a versatile and intuitive deep learning framework that leverages dynamic computation graphs, allowing real-time modification of models and simplifying debugging and experimentation processes.

✓ The framework supports a range of Machine Learning tasks, with modules such as Autograd for automatic differentiation, nn for defining neural networks, and utilities for handling large datasets efficiently.

✓ TorchVision, TorchText, and Torchaudio extend PyTorch's capabilities into specialized domains, enabling tasks in computer vision, Natural Language Processing, and audio processing through pre-built models and data manipulation tools.

✓ Dynamic computation graphs and seamless GPU acceleration make PyTorch particularly suitable for complex workflows, including reinforcement learning and tasks requiring flexible input structures like recursive networks.

- ✓ PyTorch is extensively employed in generative modeling, with architectures like GANs and VAEs facilitating advancements in image generation, anomaly detection, and artistic style transfer.
- ✓ Its integration with Hugging Face Transformers and compatibility with Python libraries make PyTorch a robust tool for implementing state-of-the-art NLP models and optimizing Machine Learning pipelines.
- ✓ With a strong focus on research and production readiness, PyTorch has become a go-to framework for both experimental and real-world deep learning applications.

Exercises

Exercise 1 – Multiple Choice Questions

1. What is the key feature of PyTorch that differentiates it from static graph-based frameworks?

   a) Pre-trained Models b) Dynamic Computation Graph

   c) Static Computation Graph d) Built-in Visualization Tools

2. Which PyTorch library is specifically designed for computer vision tasks?

   a) TorchText b) TorchVision c) Torchaudio d) TorchGraph

Exercise 2 – One Word Answers

1. What module in PyTorch is used for automatic differentiation?
2. Name the Python library that integrates PyTorch for state-of-the-art NLP models.

Exercise 3 – Short Answers

1. What is the significance of dynamic computation graphs in PyTorch?
2. Why is PyTorch widely used in reinforcement learning?

Exercise 4 – Long Answers

1. Explain the role of TorchVision in computer vision tasks with examples.
2. Discuss how PyTorch supports generative models like GANs and VAEs.

Answers

Exercise 1- 1) b, 2) b

Exercise 2- 1) Autograd, 2) Hugging Face Transformers

Online Resources

	Practice Paper	YouTube Video Playlist Link
Link	https://forms.gle/xUiqwj47ZqqjuigH6	https://www.youtube.com/playlist?list=PLzlh_31VWEFqsqyFcxRVxtgx0ZsedIlRk
QR Code		

Notes

Notes

Additional Resources

Additional Resources

In this book

Dive into the transformative world of Large Language Models (LLMs) with this comprehensive exploration, meticulously crafted to illuminate every aspect of their development, Fine-tuning, and deployment. This chapter takes you beyond the rudimentary understanding of pretrained models, delving deep into the intricate process of instruction Fine-tuning, a pivotal step in tailoring LLMs to excel in real-world, task-specific scenarios. Beginning with an insightful introduction to the fundamentals of instruction datasets, the chapter meticulously guides the reader through the nuances of dataset preparation, emphasizing the importance of input-output pair curation and contextual structuring. It underscores the art of transforming vast, unstructured textual data into meticulously organized instruction datasets capable of instilling task-specific capabilities into the model. The text seamlessly transitions into the technical domains, explaining the intricacies of custom data batching, tokenization, and collate functions, enabling the optimization of training processes for computational efficiency and precision. A detailed walkthrough of loading pretrained models showcases the power of leveraging existing architectures while ensuring compatibility with advanced Fine-tuning techniques.

Furthermore, the chapter delves into the essence of supervised Fine-tuning, weaving together the theoretical principles and practical applications of model adaptation to follow instructions with unparalleled accuracy. Through rigorous evaluation using automated tools, including state-of-the-art models like Llama 3, the text exemplifies the journey from manual benchmarking to scalable, objective performance metrics, offering readers a holistic perspective on model evaluation.

YouTube Videos Playlists for all Chapters

	Chapter 1	Chapter 2	Chapter 3	Chapter 4	Chapter 5
Link	https://www.youtube.com/playlist?list=PLzlh_31VWEFoCv8A0fBY2xgxterPZzpep	https://www.youtube.com/playlist?list=PLzlh_31VWEFq78f32uTDuWxcVpT088H6L	https://www.youtube.com/playlist?list=PLzlh_31VWEFphPBuf2Ag5MChsJdD3glV9	https://www.youtube.com/playlist?list=PLzlh_31VWEFrx4iofs2Tf6_dUsdDfRESL	https://www.youtube.com/playlist?list=PLzlh_31VWEFrqpMY3KmbBtfr8NwohTgfz
QR Code					

	Chapter 6	Chapter 7	Chapter 8
Link	https://www.youtube.com/playlist?list=PLzlh_31VWEFoDAL0w66iI-aLkpQ9E-Wcw	https://www.youtube.com/playlist?list=PLzlh_31VWEFrErzm4fzFcG6sk5USbVF-I	https://www.youtube.com/playlist?list=PLzlh_31VWEFqsqyFcxRVxtgx0ZsedIlRk
QR Code			

For Books on following Subjects

- Business, Management & Finance
- Career Development, Career Guides
- Catering & Hotel Management / Recipes
- Civil Engineering
- Computers
- Communication
- Dental / Health / Medical
- Economics
- Electrical Engineering
- Electronics & Communication
- English
- Entrepreneurship
- Environmental Engineering
- Event Management
- Fiction
- Forensic Science
- General Titles
- HRD
- International Trade
- Law
- Learning Disability
- Mathematics
- Mechanical Engineering
- Media
- Mobile Computing
- Motivation & Self Help
- Parenting
- Patent
- Physics
- Project Management / Software Engineering
- Real Estate
- Statistics

Publishers We Represent

O'REILLY®

THE X TEAM

BEP BUSINESS EXPERT PRESS

FRANKLIN, BEEDLE

Kt. Academy

Learn Coding Fast — Now everyone can learn to code

RMC LEARNING SOLUTIONS

The Pragmatic Engineer

IT REVOLUTION

Pragmatic Bookshelf

ByteByteGo

Matt Harrison

Guido van Rossum

Rheinwerk Computing

STATQUEST! TRIPLE BAM!!!

Nathan Hunter

Make: Community

sitepoint

nigelpoulton

TOWARDS AI

JORGE BRASIL